Rust for Embedded Systems

James Oakton

Published by Northwood Lore Books, 2024.

RUST FOR EMBEDDED SYSTEMS

First edition. November 18, 2024.

ISBN: 979-8230765264

Written by James Oakton.

Table of Contents

1. Introduction to Embedded Rust

Embedded systems development has traditionally been dominated by C and C++, languages that offer low level control and direct hardware access but come with significant risks in terms of memory safety and security. As our world becomes increasingly connected through the Internet of Things (IoT) and smart devices proliferate in both consumer and industrial applications, the need for a more robust and secure approach to embedded programming has never been more critical. Enter Rust, a modern systems programming language that promises to revolutionize how we build embedded applications by combining low level control with guaranteed memory safety and zero cost abstractions.

In this opening chapter, we'll explore what makes Rust particularly well suited for embedded systems development and lay the groundwork for the practical journey ahead. Rust's core premise is preventing entire classes of bugs at compile time through its ownership system, while still providing the performance and control needed for resource constrained environments. This is especially valuable in embedded systems, where bugs can be particularly difficult to debug and where security vulnerabilities can have serious real world consequences.

Embedded systems present unique challenges that set them apart from traditional software development. These systems often operate with limited resources, have real time constraints, and must interact directly with hardware through registers and memory mapped interfaces. They frequently run without an operating system, in what's known as a bare metal environment, where there's no safety net of process isolation or memory protection. In such environments, a single bug can crash the entire system or, worse, create security vulnerabilities that could be exploited in networked devices.

The embedded landscape itself is incredibly diverse, ranging from simple 8 bit microcontrollers running simple tasks to powerful systems on chip (SoC) running complex applications. Throughout this book, we'll work with several popular platforms including Arduino, STM32, and Raspberry Pi, each representing different points along this spectrum. These platforms will serve as practical examples to demonstrate Rust's capabilities in real world embedded applications.

What makes Rust particularly interesting for embedded development is its unique combination of safety features and zero cost abstractions. The ownership and borrowing system enforces strict rules about how memory can be accessed and shared between different parts of a program. This prevents common issues like buffer overflows, use after free bugs, and data races at compile time, without adding any runtime overhead. For embedded systems, where every cycle and byte counts, this combination of safety and efficiency is invaluable.

Rust's type system and trait based generics enable powerful abstractions that can be completely resolved at compile time, resulting in code that's both safe and efficient. The embedded hal (Hardware Abstraction Layer) ecosystem leverages these features to provide portable interfaces for common peripheral types, allowing developers to write platform independent code while still maintaining direct hardware control when needed.

Throughout this book, we'll explore how to leverage these features in practical embedded applications. We'll start with the basics of setting up a development environment and understanding fundamental concepts, then progress to increasingly sophisticated projects that demonstrate real world applications. You'll learn how to work with various peripherals, implement common communication protocols, manage resources efficiently, and build secure, reliable IoT devices.

One of the most significant advantages of using Rust for embedded development is its growing ecosystem of tools and libraries specifically designed for embedded systems. The embedded hal ecosystem provides a standardized way to interact with hardware peripherals, while tools like probe run and defmt make debugging and logging more convenient than ever. The Rust compiler's strong guarantees help catch many issues before code ever runs on hardware, significantly reducing debugging time and improving reliability.

Security is a particular focus throughout this book, as IoT devices have become frequent targets for cyber attacks. Rust's safety guarantees provide a strong foundation for building secure systems, but we'll also explore additional security best practices, secure communication protocols, and techniques for implementing secure boot and over the air updates. These are critical considerations for any modern embedded system connected to networks.

Real time capabilities are essential for many embedded applications, and we'll explore how Rust can be used effectively in such contexts. While Rust's safety guarantees do introduce some considerations for real time programming, we'll see how to work within these constraints while still maintaining predictable timing behavior. We'll examine both bare metal real time programming and the use of real time operating systems (RTOS) with Rust.

As we progress through the book, you'll gain hands on experience with increasingly complex projects. We'll start with simple examples like blinking LEDs and reading sensors, then move on to more sophisticated applications like motor control systems, data loggers, and IoT gateways. Each project will introduce new concepts while reinforcing fundamental principles of embedded Rust development.

While this book assumes some familiarity with programming concepts, you don't need prior experience with Rust or embedded systems. If you're coming from a C or C++ background, you'll find many familiar concepts, but presented with Rust's unique approach to safety and abstraction. We'll take time to explain Rust specific concepts as they become relevant to our embedded programming journey.

The embedded systems field is rapidly evolving, with new hardware platforms and requirements emerging constantly. Rust's growing ecosystem and active community make it well positioned to address these challenges. By the end of this book, you'll have the knowledge and skills needed to develop secure, reliable embedded applications using Rust, whether you're working on simple microcontroller projects or complex IoT systems.

In the chapters that follow, we'll dive deep into specific aspects of embedded Rust development, from low level hardware interaction to high level application architecture. Each chapter builds on previous concepts while introducing new techniques and best practices. The journey begins with understanding why Rust is particularly well suited for embedded development, then progresses through practical implementation details to advanced topics in security, optimization, and deployment.

Remember that embedded development often requires patience and attention to detail. Take time to understand the concepts presented, experiment with the example code, and don't hesitate to explore beyond the provided examples. The skills you'll develop throughout this book will serve as a foundation for building robust, secure embedded systems in Rust.

2. Why Rust for Embedded Systems

The decision to use Rust for embedded systems development represents a significant shift from traditional approaches, and it's important to understand the compelling reasons behind this choice. Rust brings a unique combination of safety, performance, and modern language features that make it particularly well suited for the challenges of embedded development.

First and foremost, Rust's commitment to memory safety without runtime overhead addresses one of the most critical challenges in embedded systems development. Traditional languages like C and C++ provide the low level control necessary for embedded programming, but they also make it easy to introduce memory related bugs that can be devastating in an embedded context. Buffer overflows, use after free errors, and data races are just a few examples of issues that can lead to system crashes, unpredictable behavior, or security vulnerabilities. Rust's ownership system and borrow checker catch these issues at compile time, ensuring that such bugs never make it to production hardware.

The zero cost nature of Rust's safety guarantees is particularly important in the resource constrained world of embedded systems. Unlike languages that rely on garbage collection or runtime checks, Rust's safety features are enforced entirely at compile time. This means you get the benefits of memory safety without paying any performance penalty or increasing memory usage. For embedded systems where every byte of RAM and every CPU cycle counts, this is a crucial advantage.

Rust's type system and trait based abstractions provide powerful tools for writing clear, maintainable code without sacrificing performance. The ability to create zero cost abstractions means you can write high level, expressive code that compiles down to the same efficient machine code you'd get from writing low level C. This is particularly valuable in embedded systems where you often need to balance the need for clear, maintainable code with strict performance requirements.

Another significant advantage of Rust for embedded development is its strong support for concurrent programming. Many modern embedded systems, particularly in IoT applications, need to handle multiple tasks simultaneously, such as processing sensor data while maintaining network connections. Rust's ownership system makes it impossible to create data races at compile time, while its async/await syntax provides elegant tools for handling concurrent operations. This is a massive improvement over the error prone approach to concurrency in traditional embedded programming.

The Rust ecosystem has developed robust tools specifically for embedded development. The embedded hal ecosystem provides a standardized way to interact with hardware peripherals, making it possible to write portable code that works across different microcontrollers. Tools like probe run and defmt make debugging and logging more convenient than traditional approaches. The cargo build system and package manager make it easy to manage dependencies and build configurations, while still maintaining the fine grained control needed for embedded development.

Security considerations are becoming increasingly important in embedded systems, particularly with the growth of IoT devices. Rust's safety guarantees provide a strong foundation for building secure systems by eliminating entire classes of vulnerabilities at compile time. Memory corruption bugs, which are a common source of security vulnerabilities in C and C++ code, are simply impossible in safe Rust code. While it's still possible to write insecure applications in Rust, the language provides strong guardrails that make it much easier to write secure code by default.

Resource management is another area where Rust shines in embedded development. The ownership system provides clear rules for managing resources, whether that's memory, hardware peripherals, or other system resources. This is particularly valuable in embedded systems where resources are limited and proper cleanup is critical. Rust's RAII (Resource Acquisition Is Initialization) pattern ensures that resources are properly initialized and cleaned up, even in error cases.

The learning curve of Rust is often cited as a potential drawback, but this investment pays dividends in embedded development. While it may take time to understand concepts like ownership and borrowing, these same concepts prevent countless hours of debugging memory issues and tracking down hard to reproduce bugs. The compiler becomes a helpful assistant, catching potential issues before they become runtime problems.

Rust's strong type system and pattern matching capabilities make it easier to handle error conditions robustly, which is crucial in embedded systems where graceful error handling can be the difference between a minor glitch and a complete system failure. The Option and Result types force explicit handling of error cases and null values, preventing many common sources of runtime errors.

The language's support for unsafe code, when necessary, provides an escape hatch for cases where the strict safety guarantees need to be bypassed. This is particularly important in embedded development where direct hardware access and bit manipulation are often required. However, unsafe code is clearly marked and isolated, making it easier to audit and maintain compared to languages where all code is potentially unsafe.

Rust's growing community and ecosystem provide another compelling reason for its use in embedded systems. The language has a active community of developers working on embedded specific tools and libraries, and the pace of improvement in this area is rapid.

Regular releases of the language bring new features and improvements that benefit embedded developers, while maintaining strong backwards compatibility.

Cross platform development is well supported in Rust, making it easier to develop for different target architectures. The cargo build system handles cross compilation smoothly, and the standard library can be easily excluded for bare metal development. This makes it practical to maintain a single codebase that can target different platforms, from simple microcontrollers to more powerful systems.

Performance optimization is well supported in Rust, with tools for examining generated assembly code and measuring performance. The language provides fine grained control over memory layout and alignment, which can be crucial for optimizing embedded applications. The ability to eliminate runtime overhead through zero cost abstractions means you can write clear, maintainable code without sacrificing performance.

Looking to the future, Rust's momentum in the embedded space continues to grow. Major companies are adopting Rust for embedded development, and the ecosystem of tools and libraries continues to expand. The language's emphasis on safety and performance aligns well with the increasing demands for secure, reliable embedded systems, particularly in IoT and industrial applications.

The choice of Rust for embedded development represents a forward thinking approach that addresses many of the traditional challenges in embedded programming while providing modern language features and tools. While there may be a learning curve, the benefits in terms of safety, reliability, and maintainability make it an increasingly attractive choice for embedded systems development.

3. Setting Up Your Development Environment

Setting up a proper development environment is crucial for successful embedded systems development with Rust. This chapter will guide you through the process of establishing a robust development setup that will serve as the foundation for your embedded Rust projects.

The first step in setting up your development environment is installing Rust itself. The recommended way to install Rust is through rustup, the official Rust toolchain installer. Rustup makes it easy to install and manage different versions of Rust and provides essential tools like cargo, the Rust package manager. To install rustup, visit rustup.rs and follow the installation instructions for your operating system. On Unix-like systems, you can typically install it with a simple curl command, while Windows users can download and run the rustup installer.

Once you have rustup installed, you'll need to install the appropriate target architecture for your embedded development. Rust supports a wide range of target architectures through cross compilation. For example, if you're working with ARM-based microcontrollers, you might need to add the ARM Cortex-M targets. This can be done using the rustup target add command. Common targets include thumbv6m-none-eabi for ARM Cortex-M0 and M0+, thumbv7m-none-eabi for Cortex-M3, and thumbv7em-none-eabi for Cortex-M4 and M7.

A good IDE or text editor setup is essential for productive Rust development. Visual Studio Code with the rust-analyzer extension provides an excellent development experience. Rust-analyzer offers features like code completion, go to definition, real-time error checking, and more. Other popular choices include CLion with the

Rust plugin, which provides robust debugging support, or Vim/Neovim with appropriate Rust plugins for those who prefer terminal-based editors.

For debugging embedded systems, you'll need appropriate hardware debugging tools. The most common option is a JTAG/SWD debugger. Popular choices include the ST-Link (particularly for STM32 development), J-Link from SEGGER, or the Black Magic Probe. These debuggers allow you to flash your program to the target device, set breakpoints, and inspect variables during program execution. Make sure to install the appropriate drivers and software for your chosen debugger.

The probe-run tool is particularly useful for embedded development as it provides a more user-friendly debugging experience. It allows you to run your embedded program directly from the command line and provides better error messages than traditional debugging tools. You can install probe-run using cargo install probe-run. Similarly, flip-link is useful for optimizing the memory layout of your programs, and can be installed with cargo install flip-link.

For logging and debugging output, the defmt framework provides a excellent solution for embedded systems. It offers compile-time formatting checks and efficient logging without requiring a heap or dynamic memory allocation. Install it by adding it as a dependency in your project's Cargo.toml file.

When working with specific microcontroller families, you'll often need additional tools. For STM32 development, the STM32CubeProgrammer is useful for device programming and flash memory manipulation. Arduino development might require the arduino-cli tool for board management. These platform-specific tools complement the core Rust toolchain and provide necessary functionality for working with specific hardware.

Version control is essential for any software development project, and embedded Rust is no exception. Git is the standard choice for version control. Make sure to set up Git on your system and configure it with your credentials. It's also worth setting up a .gitignore file appropriate for Rust projects, which should exclude target directories, build artifacts, and any IDE-specific files.

For building and testing your embedded projects, you'll want to set up a consistent build environment. Create a template project structure that includes appropriate target configurations in .cargo/config.toml, any necessary memory layout files (linker scripts), and a suitable Cargo.toml with common dependencies. This template can serve as a starting point for new projects and help maintain consistency across different projects.

Documentation tools are another important aspect of your development environment. Rustdoc, which comes with Rust, generates documentation from your code comments. Consider setting up a documentation generation pipeline that builds and publishes documentation for your projects. This is particularly important for team projects or open source contributions.

Continuous integration (CI) tools can help ensure your code remains working as you make changes. GitHub Actions or GitLab CI can be configured to build and test your embedded Rust projects automatically. Setting up CI early in your project can catch issues before they become problems and help maintain code quality.

The cargo generate tool is useful for creating new projects from templates. You can install it with cargo install cargo-generate. This tool makes it easy to start new projects with all the necessary configuration and boilerplate code already in place. Consider creating your own template repository with your preferred project structure and configurations.

For testing embedded code, you'll want to set up both unit testing capabilities and hardware-in-the-loop testing where appropriate. The embedded-hal-mock crate is useful for writing tests that simulate hardware behavior without requiring actual hardware. Consider setting up a test hardware configuration that allows for automated testing of your embedded code.

Package management in Rust is handled through Cargo and crates.io, but you might want to set up a local cache or mirror of commonly used crates, especially in corporate environments where internet access might be restricted. Cargo's configuration allows you to specify alternative registry sources and local caches.

When working with multiple projects or different versions of tools, it can be helpful to use virtual environments or containerization. Docker can be particularly useful for creating reproducible build environments, especially when working with complex toolchains or when collaboration across different development platforms is required.

Finally, consider setting up a systematic way to organize your project workspaces. A well-organized workspace might include separate directories for different types of projects (e.g., Arduino, STM32, Raspberry Pi), shared libraries, and documentation. Having a consistent organization scheme makes it easier to manage multiple projects and share code between them.

Remember that your development environment will evolve as you work on different projects and as new tools become available. Regularly review and update your setup, and keep track of your configuration in version control so you can easily recreate your development environment when needed. Consider documenting your setup process and maintaining a list of required tools and their versions to help onboard new team members or set up new development machines.

4. Understanding Embedded Hardware Basics

Understanding embedded hardware basics is fundamental to successful embedded systems development. Before diving into Rust programming for embedded systems, it's essential to grasp the core concepts and components that make up embedded hardware platforms.

At the heart of any embedded system lies the microcontroller or processor. Unlike general purpose computers, microcontrollers integrate multiple components into a single chip, including the processor core, memory, and various peripherals. The processor core executes instructions and performs calculations, while different types of memory store program code and data. Most modern embedded systems use ARM architecture processors, particularly the Cortex M series, though there are many other architectures like RISC V, AVR, and PIC.

Memory in embedded systems is typically divided into several types, each serving different purposes. Flash memory stores the program code and constant data, and retains its contents even when power is removed. RAM (Random Access Memory) provides temporary storage for variables and the program stack during execution. Some systems also include EEPROM for storing configuration data that needs to be retained but might change occasionally. Understanding these memory types is crucial because embedded systems often have very limited memory resources, requiring careful consideration of memory usage in your programs.

The clock system is another critical component of embedded hardware. The system clock determines how fast instructions are executed and coordinates various peripheral operations. Most microcontrollers have multiple clock sources, including external crystal oscillators for precise timing, and internal RC oscillators for lower power operation. Clock configuration affects both system performance and power consumption, making it an important consideration in embedded system design.

Peripherals are specialized hardware modules that handle specific functions. GPIO (General Purpose Input/Output) pins allow the microcontroller to interact with the external world through digital signals. These pins can be configured as inputs to read external signals or outputs to control external devices. Many pins can serve multiple functions, being multiplexed between different peripherals.

Communication interfaces are essential peripherals in most embedded systems. UART (Universal Asynchronous Receiver/Transmitter) provides serial communication capabilities, useful for debugging and communicating with other devices. I2C (Inter Integrated Circuit) and SPI (Serial Peripheral Interface) are synchronous protocols commonly used to communicate with sensors, displays, and other peripheral devices. Each of these interfaces has its own characteristics and trade offs in terms of speed, complexity, and number of required pins.

Timer peripherals are used for precise timing operations and generating periodic events. They can be used for tasks like measuring time intervals, generating PWM (Pulse Width Modulation) signals for motor control or LED brightness adjustment, or triggering periodic interrupts. Most microcontrollers provide multiple timer modules with various capabilities.

Analog interfaces allow the microcontroller to interact with analog signals from the real world. ADC (Analog to Digital Converter) modules convert analog voltages into digital values that can be processed by the microcontroller. DAC (Digital to Analog Converter) modules perform the opposite conversion, generating analog voltages from digital values. Some microcontrollers also include analog comparators for comparing voltage levels.

Power management is a crucial aspect of embedded systems. Most microcontrollers offer various power saving modes, allowing portions of the system to be shut down when not needed. Understanding these power modes and how to properly transition between them is important for creating energy efficient systems, particularly for battery powered devices.

The reset system ensures the microcontroller starts up in a known state and can recover from software errors. Reset sources might include power on reset, external reset pins, watchdog timers, and software reset capabilities. The startup sequence, including clock initialization and peripheral setup, is critical for proper system operation.

Debug interfaces provide means to program and debug the microcontroller. Common interfaces include JTAG (Joint Test Action Group) and SWD (Serial Wire Debug), which allow programming the device, setting breakpoints, and examining memory and registers during program execution. Understanding these interfaces is essential for development and troubleshooting.

Protection mechanisms are built into many microcontrollers to prevent accidental or malicious modification of critical system settings. These might include write protection for flash memory, security features to prevent unauthorized access to debug interfaces, and memory protection units to prevent errant software from corrupting critical memory regions.

External components often complement the microcontroller to create a complete embedded system. These might include voltage regulators for power supply, external memory chips for additional storage, real time clock modules for time keeping, and various sensors and actuators. Understanding how to interface with these components and their requirements is important for system design.

PCB (Printed Circuit Board) design considerations are also important when working with embedded systems. This includes understanding proper power supply decoupling, signal integrity requirements, and EMI (Electromagnetic Interference) considerations. While software developers might not be directly involved in PCB design, understanding these aspects helps in debugging hardware related issues and writing more robust code.

System level considerations include bootloader operation, firmware update mechanisms, and fault tolerance features. Many embedded systems need to be able to update their firmware in the field, requiring careful consideration of the bootloader design and update process. Fault tolerance features might include watchdog timers, error detection and correction in memory, and redundant systems for critical applications.

Understanding the constraints and capabilities of embedded hardware helps in writing more efficient and reliable code. Memory constraints might influence algorithm choices and data structure design. Peripheral capabilities and limitations affect how you implement various features. Power consumption considerations might influence how you structure your program's main loop and use of sleep modes.

Documentation is a critical resource when working with embedded hardware. This includes microcontroller datasheets, reference manuals, application notes, and hardware schematics. Learning to effectively read and understand this documentation is an essential skill for embedded systems development.

5. Rust's Memory Safety Features in Embedded Context

Memory safety is one of Rust's most compelling features, and its significance becomes even more pronounced in embedded systems development where memory errors can have severe consequences. In embedded systems, there's no operating system to catch and handle memory errors gracefully, making Rust's compile time guarantees particularly valuable.

Rust's ownership system forms the foundation of its memory safety guarantees. In embedded systems, where resources are limited and direct hardware access is common, understanding how ownership works becomes crucial. Each value in Rust has a single owner at any given time, and when the owner goes out of scope, the value is automatically deallocated. This prevents common issues like use after free bugs, which can be particularly problematic in embedded systems where memory corruption might lead to system failures or security vulnerabilities.

The borrow checker, Rust's compile time enforcement mechanism, ensures that references to data are valid and prevents data races. In embedded systems, where concurrent access to hardware registers is common, this becomes particularly important. The borrow checker ensures that while multiple immutable references to data can exist simultaneously, only one mutable reference is allowed at a time. This rule applies not just to regular variables but also to hardware registers accessed through memory mapped I/O.

Static allocation plays a significant role in embedded Rust programming. Unlike desktop applications where dynamic memory allocation is common, embedded systems often avoid dynamic allocation due to resource constraints and reliability requirements.

Rust's support for static allocation through const declarations and static variables aligns well with these requirements. The compiler ensures that static variables are properly initialized before use, preventing undefined behavior that could occur with uninitialized variables in C or C++.

Zero sized types in Rust provide a powerful abstraction mechanism without runtime overhead. This is particularly valuable in embedded systems where every byte of memory counts. For example, you can use zero sized types to represent hardware capabilities or states at compile time, ensuring that certain operations are only possible when the appropriate hardware features are available, all without consuming any runtime memory.

Rust's enum type provides a memory efficient way to represent variants, which is particularly useful in embedded systems. Unlike C enums, Rust enums can contain data and are guaranteed to be properly sized and aligned. This makes them ideal for representing different states of hardware peripherals or communication protocols. The compiler ensures exhaustive matching of enum variants, preventing bugs that could occur from unhandled cases.

The Option type in Rust eliminates null pointer dereferencing, a common source of crashes in embedded systems. Instead of using null pointers, Rust requires explicit handling of optional values through the Option enum. This is particularly valuable when dealing with hardware peripherals that might or might not be present, or when handling potentially failing operations.

Error handling in embedded Rust leverages the Result type, providing a systematic way to handle errors without exceptions. This is crucial in embedded systems where exception handling might not be available or might be too costly in terms of code size and runtime overhead. The Result type forces explicit error handling, making the code more robust and easier to reason about.

Memory mapped I/O is a fundamental aspect of embedded systems programming, and Rust provides safe abstractions for working with it. Through the volatile_read and volatile_write operations, Rust ensures that accesses to hardware registers are not optimized away by the compiler. The type system can be used to ensure that hardware registers are accessed with the correct data types and alignment requirements.

Rust's support for unsafe blocks provides a controlled way to implement low level operations that cannot be proved safe by the compiler. This is often necessary in embedded systems when directly accessing hardware or implementing device drivers. However, unsafe blocks must be explicitly marked, making it clear where the programmer takes responsibility for maintaining safety invariants. This helps contain potentially unsafe operations and makes code reviews more focused.

The concept of Send and Sync traits becomes particularly important when dealing with interrupts and concurrent access to hardware. These traits ensure that types can be safely shared between different execution contexts. For example, a type that represents a hardware peripheral might implement Send to indicate it can be safely moved to an interrupt handler, while implementing Sync would allow it to be safely shared between multiple contexts.

Buffer management in embedded systems often requires careful control over memory layout and alignment. Rust's repr attributes and packed structs provide fine grained control over memory layout while maintaining safety guarantees. This is essential when working with DMA transfers or implementing communication protocols with specific memory layout requirements.

Rust's lifetime system ensures that references remain valid for their entire intended use. This is particularly valuable when dealing with hardware buffers or DMA operations where the lifetime of data must be carefully managed. The compiler will prevent cases where data might be invalidated while still in use by hardware operations.

The type system can be leveraged to create zero cost abstractions that enforce hardware specific constraints. For example, you can create types that represent specific peripheral states, ensuring that operations are only possible when the peripheral is in the correct state. These abstractions are resolved at compile time, adding no runtime overhead while providing strong safety guarantees.

Rust's const generics feature allows for compile time validation of buffer sizes and other numeric parameters. This is particularly useful in embedded systems where buffer sizes often need to match hardware requirements. The compiler can ensure that only valid sizes are used, preventing runtime errors that could occur from mismatched buffer sizes.

Memory initialization is another area where Rust's safety features shine. The compiler ensures that variables are properly initialized before use, preventing undefined behavior that could occur from reading uninitialized memory. This is particularly important in embedded systems where memory contents might be undefined after power up.

The Drop trait provides deterministic cleanup of resources, which is crucial in embedded systems where resource management must be predictable. This can be used to ensure that hardware peripherals are properly disabled when no longer needed, or that shared resources are properly released.

Atomic operations in Rust provide safe mechanisms for sharing data between different execution contexts, such as between the main program and interrupt handlers. The compiler ensures that atomic operations are properly synchronized, preventing data races that could lead to undefined behavior.

While Rust's safety features might seem restrictive at first, they actually enable more confident and robust embedded systems development. The compile time checks catch many common errors before they can manifest as runtime issues, which is particularly valuable in embedded systems where debugging can be challenging and failures can be costly.

These safety features don't come at the cost of performance or control. Through careful design of its type system and zero cost abstractions, Rust provides these safety guarantees while still allowing fine grained control over hardware resources and maintaining the performance characteristics required for embedded systems.

6. Bare Metal Programming Fundamentals

Chapter 6 focuses on the fundamental aspects of bare metal programming in Rust, providing developers with essential knowledge for working directly with microcontroller hardware without an operating system.

Bare metal programming represents the most direct way to interact with embedded hardware, where your code runs directly on the processor without any operating system intermediary. In Rust, this approach requires careful consideration of hardware initialization, resource management, and program structure.

At the heart of bare metal programming lies the concept of the entry point. Unlike standard Rust programs that begin with main(), bare metal applications typically start with a custom entry point marked with #[entry]. This function is responsible for the initial setup of the hardware and serves as the starting point for your application. The entry point must never return, as there's no operating system to return to, usually implementing an infinite loop that contains the main application logic.

Memory management in bare metal programming requires special attention. Without an operating system, you're responsible for setting up the stack and managing memory regions. Rust's memory safety features are particularly valuable here, helping prevent common errors that could lead to system crashes. The linker script plays a crucial role in defining memory layouts, specifying where different sections of your program will be placed in memory.

Hardware initialization is a critical aspect of bare metal programming. Before your application can run effectively, you need to configure various system clocks, enable peripheral clocks, and set up initial states for hardware peripherals. Rust provides safe abstractions for these operations through hardware abstraction layers (HALs) and peripheral access crates (PACs), but understanding the underlying initialization requirements remains essential.

Vector tables represent another fundamental concept in bare metal programming. These tables contain the addresses of exception and interrupt handlers that the processor will jump to when specific events occur. In Rust, we typically define these using static arrays with function pointers, ensuring type safety while maintaining the low level control necessary for embedded systems.

Register access forms the foundation of bare metal programming, allowing direct interaction with hardware peripherals. Rust provides safe abstractions through volatile reads and writes, ensuring that compiler optimizations don't interfere with hardware interactions. Memory mapped I/O (MMIO) is handled through special types that enforce proper access patterns while maintaining safety guarantees.

Critical sections become important when dealing with shared resources and interrupts in bare metal programming. Rust's type system helps ensure that critical sections are properly managed, preventing race conditions and other synchronization issues. The critical section API typically involves disabling interrupts temporarily while accessing shared resources.

Resource management in bare metal programming requires careful attention to initialization and deinitialization sequences. Rust's RAII (Resource Acquisition Is Initialization) pattern works well here, allowing you to tie resource lifetimes to scope boundaries. This helps ensure that resources are properly cleaned up, even in error conditions.

Startup code plays a vital role in bare metal applications, handling tasks like initializing the stack pointer, copying initialized data from flash to RAM, and zeroing the BSS section. While much of this is handled by the runtime crate, understanding these operations helps when debugging initialization issues or customizing the startup sequence.

Debugging bare metal applications presents unique challenges, as traditional debugging tools might not be available. Rust's strong type system helps catch many issues at compile time, but hardware debuggers and JTAG interfaces become essential tools for runtime debugging. Understanding how to set up and use these tools effectively is crucial for bare metal development.

Exception handling in bare metal programming requires careful consideration, as there's no operating system to catch and handle unexpected conditions. Rust's panic handler must be customized for bare metal applications, typically implementing a minimal handler that can safely halt the system or perform recovery operations.

Power management becomes particularly important in bare metal applications, where you have direct control over the processor's power states. Rust's type system can help ensure that power state transitions are handled correctly, preventing undefined behavior that could occur from improper state management.

Timing and delays in bare metal programming often rely on hardware timers or cycle counting. Rust provides safe abstractions for these operations while maintaining precise control over timing. Understanding how to implement accurate delays without relying on operating system services is essential.

The build process for bare metal applications requires special consideration. Custom target specifications might be needed to define the appropriate CPU architecture and features. The cargo build system needs to be configured with appropriate linker scripts and build flags to generate correct binary outputs for the target hardware.

Memory constraints in bare metal programming often require careful optimization of code size and RAM usage. Rust's zero cost abstractions help here, allowing you to write high level code that compiles down to efficient machine code. Understanding how to use features like const generics and inline assembly when necessary helps optimize resource usage.

Testing bare metal code presents unique challenges, as traditional unit testing approaches might not be directly applicable. Hardware in the loop testing becomes important, and understanding how to structure code to enable testing of individual components helps maintain code quality.

Documentation becomes particularly important in bare metal programming, where the relationship between software and hardware must be clearly understood. Rust's documentation tools help maintain clear documentation of hardware requirements and initialization sequences.

As you progress in bare metal programming, understanding how to implement various communication protocols becomes essential. This includes both internal protocols for peripheral communication and external protocols for system interaction. Rust's type system helps ensure protocol implementations remain correct and safe.

The journey into bare metal programming with Rust provides a solid foundation for building more complex embedded systems. The principles learned here apply whether you're working with simple microcontrollers or more complex systems with multiple peripherals and communication interfaces.

7. Real-Time Operating System Concepts

Real-time operating systems (RTOS) form a crucial component in many embedded systems, providing predictable timing behavior and efficient resource management for time-critical applications. Unlike general purpose operating systems, an RTOS prioritizes deterministic behavior and rapid response times over raw throughput or user interface convenience.

At its core, an RTOS manages multiple tasks or threads, scheduling them according to their priorities and timing requirements. The key characteristic that distinguishes an RTOS from a general purpose operating system is its ability to guarantee response times for critical tasks. This predictability is essential in applications like industrial automation, medical devices, or automotive systems where missed deadlines could have serious consequences.

Task scheduling in an RTOS typically follows priority-based algorithms. The scheduler ensures that the highest priority ready task always gets CPU time, implementing what's known as preemptive scheduling. When a high priority task becomes ready to run, it can immediately preempt a lower priority task, ensuring critical operations receive immediate attention. Rust's ownership and borrowing rules help ensure that task switching occurs safely, preventing data races and other concurrency issues.

Time management forms another fundamental aspect of RTOS operation. Most RTOS implementations provide both time-delay functions and timeout mechanisms. These allow tasks to sleep for specific durations or wait for events with timeout constraints. The resolution and accuracy of these timing functions depend on the system timer configuration and the RTOS implementation. Rust's strong type system helps enforce correct usage of timing APIs, preventing common errors like overflow or underflow in time calculations.

Inter-task communication mechanisms are essential RTOS features that allow tasks to coordinate their activities. These typically include message queues, semaphores, mutexes, and event flags. Message queues enable tasks to exchange data safely, while semaphores and mutexes provide synchronization primitives. Event flags allow tasks to signal conditions to each other efficiently. Rust's ownership model naturally extends to these communication mechanisms, ensuring thread-safe access to shared resources.

Memory management in an RTOS environment requires careful consideration. Many RTOS implementations provide memory allocation services, but these must be deterministic to maintain real-time behavior. Fixed-size memory pools are common, allowing predictable allocation times. Rust's compile-time memory management helps here, as many allocations can be resolved at compile time, reducing runtime overhead and improving predictability.

Priority inversion represents a common challenge in RTOS design, occurring when a high priority task is indirectly blocked by a lower priority task. Most RTOS implementations provide priority inheritance mechanisms to address this issue. When a high priority task waits for a resource held by a lower priority task, the lower priority task temporarily inherits the higher priority, ensuring it can complete its critical section quickly. Rust's type system can help encode these priority relationships, making priority inversion issues easier to detect and prevent.

Resource management extends beyond CPU scheduling to include peripherals and other system resources. An RTOS typically provides mechanisms for managing shared access to hardware resources, ensuring that multiple tasks can safely interact with peripherals. Rust's ownership system naturally extends to resource management, helping prevent concurrent access issues while maintaining efficient resource utilization.

Error handling in an RTOS environment requires special consideration. Unlike desktop applications, embedded systems often can't simply crash and restart when errors occur. RTOS implementations typically provide mechanisms for error recovery and fault tolerance. Rust's Result type and error handling patterns work well here, allowing for robust error handling without runtime overhead.

Task synchronization mechanisms form another crucial aspect of RTOS functionality. These include critical sections, where interrupts may be temporarily disabled to ensure atomic operations, and various synchronization primitives like mutexes and semaphores. Rust's type system helps ensure that synchronization mechanisms are used correctly, preventing common concurrency bugs.

Power management becomes particularly important in RTOS-based systems, especially for battery-powered devices. Many RTOS implementations provide power management features, allowing tasks to influence system power states. The RTOS can coordinate power state transitions, ensuring that all tasks are appropriately notified and can prepare for power state changes. Rust's type system can help ensure that power state transitions are handled safely.

Interrupt handling in an RTOS environment requires careful coordination with the task scheduler. Interrupts typically execute at a higher priority than any task, but they must be kept short to maintain system responsiveness. The RTOS provides mechanisms for interrupts to wake tasks, allowing longer processing to occur at task level. Rust's interrupt handling abstractions work well with RTOS requirements, ensuring safe interaction between interrupts and tasks.

Debugging RTOS-based applications presents unique challenges, as timing-related issues can be difficult to reproduce and analyze. Many RTOS implementations provide debugging features like task statistics, CPU usage monitoring, and event logging. Understanding how to effectively use these features becomes crucial for developing reliable RTOS applications. Rust's strong type system helps catch many issues at compile time, reducing the need for runtime debugging.

Testing RTOS applications requires consideration of timing constraints and concurrent behavior. Unit tests must account for task interactions and timing requirements. Integration testing becomes particularly important, as the interaction between tasks can lead to complex behaviors. Rust's testing framework can be extended to support RTOS-specific testing requirements.

Documentation plays a crucial role in RTOS development, as understanding task interactions and timing requirements becomes essential for maintaining and modifying the system. Rust's documentation tools help maintain clear documentation of task priorities, resource usage, and timing constraints.

As embedded systems become more complex, understanding RTOS concepts becomes increasingly important. Whether using an existing RTOS or implementing real-time features in bare metal applications, the principles of predictable timing and efficient resource management remain crucial. Rust's safety features and zero-cost abstractions make it an excellent choice for implementing real-time systems, providing strong guarantees while maintaining the performance necessary for embedded applications.

8. The embedded-hal Ecosystem

The embedded-hal ecosystem represents one of Rust's most significant achievements in embedded systems development, providing a standardized interface for hardware abstraction across different microcontroller families. This ecosystem enables developers to write portable code that works across various hardware platforms while maintaining the performance characteristics necessary for embedded applications.

At its core, embedded-hal defines a set of traits that represent common embedded peripherals and their operations. These traits serve as contracts between hardware abstraction layer (HAL) implementations and device drivers, allowing developers to write hardware-agnostic code that can be easily ported across different platforms. The ecosystem follows Rust's zero-cost abstraction principle, ensuring that these abstractions don't introduce runtime overhead.

The foundational traits in embedded-hal cover basic digital input and output operations, serial communication protocols, timers, and analog interfaces. For example, the OutputPin trait defines the basic interface for controlling digital output pins, while InputPin handles digital inputs. These simple but powerful abstractions allow developers to write generic code that works with any microcontroller implementing these traits.

Serial communication protocols receive comprehensive coverage in the embedded-hal ecosystem. Traits exist for common protocols like I2C, SPI, and UART, defining standard interfaces for these communication methods. This standardization enables the development of platform-independent device drivers. A sensor driver written using embedded-hal traits can work unchanged across different microcontroller families, as long as appropriate HAL implementations exist for each platform.

The ecosystem extends beyond basic peripheral access to include more complex functionality. Traits exist for pulse width modulation (PWM), analog-to-digital conversion (ADC), digital-to-analog conversion (DAC), and other common embedded system features. These abstractions maintain the balance between usability and performance, ensuring that developers can write clear, maintainable code without sacrificing efficiency.

Error handling in embedded-hal follows Rust's standard patterns while accommodating the unique requirements of embedded systems. The traits use Rust's Result type to handle errors, but implementations can choose zero-cost error handling approaches suitable for resource-constrained environments. This flexibility allows developers to implement appropriate error handling strategies for their specific applications.

The embedded-hal ecosystem includes a growing collection of device drivers built on these standard traits. These drivers cover various sensors, displays, motor controllers, and other common peripheral devices. The standardized interface means that these drivers can be easily shared and reused across different projects and platforms, fostering a collaborative development environment.

Implementation of embedded hal traits requires careful consideration of hardware capabilities and limitations. HAL implementers must ensure that their implementations maintain the semantic requirements of the traits while working within the constraints of their specific hardware. This often involves balancing abstraction with access to hardware-specific features.

The blocking nature of many embedded-hal traits represents a deliberate design choice, simplifying driver implementation and usage. However, the ecosystem also includes async versions of these traits for use in more complex applications requiring non-blocking operation. This flexibility allows developers to choose the appropriate abstraction level for their specific needs.

Device driver development using embedded-hal demonstrates the power of Rust's trait system. Drivers can be written to depend only on the traits they need, making them highly portable and reusable. For example, a temperature sensor driver might only require I2C communication traits, allowing it to work with any microcontroller that implements these traits.

The ecosystem supports different levels of abstraction, from low-level register access to high-level peripheral interfaces. This layered approach allows developers to choose the appropriate abstraction level for their needs, dropping down to lower levels when necessary for performance or specific hardware features while using higher-level abstractions for simpler tasks.

Testing represents another strength of the embedded-hal ecosystem. The trait-based approach allows for easy mocking of hardware interfaces, enabling comprehensive testing of device drivers without actual hardware. This capability significantly improves the development process, allowing developers to catch issues early through automated testing.

Documentation plays a crucial role in the embedded-hal ecosystem. Trait documentation clearly specifies expected behavior, making it easier for both HAL implementers and driver developers to create correct implementations. This documentation, combined with Rust's strong type system, helps prevent many common embedded development errors.

The future of embedded-hal continues to evolve with the embedded Rust ecosystem. Ongoing developments include expanded trait coverage, improved async support, and better integration with other embedded Rust tools and frameworks. The ecosystem maintains backward compatibility while incorporating new features and improvements based on community feedback and real-world usage.

Performance considerations remain paramount in the embedded-hal ecosystem. The trait-based approach allows for efficient implementations, with most abstractions compiling down to direct hardware access. This efficiency makes embedded-hal suitable for even highly resource-constrained systems.

The embedded-hal ecosystem demonstrates the power of Rust's type system and trait-based abstraction in embedded systems development. By providing a standardized interface for hardware abstraction, it enables the development of portable, reliable embedded software while maintaining the performance characteristics necessary for embedded applications. The growing collection of device drivers and HAL implementations makes it an increasingly valuable resource for embedded Rust developers.

9. GPIO Programming in Rust

General Purpose Input/Output (GPIO) forms the foundation of most embedded systems interactions, serving as the basic interface between a microcontroller and the external world. In Rust, GPIO programming combines the language's safety guarantees with efficient, zero-cost abstractions to provide reliable control over digital pins.

At its most fundamental level, GPIO allows us to configure pins as either inputs or outputs. When configured as an output, a pin can be set to either a high state (typically representing the supply voltage) or a low state (typically ground). As an input, a pin can read the voltage level applied to it, interpreting it as either a logical high or low. Rust's type system helps enforce correct pin configuration and usage, preventing common errors like reading from pins configured as outputs or writing to input pins.

The embedded-hal traits provide a standardized interface for GPIO operations. The basic OutputPin trait defines methods for setting pins high or low, while InputPin provides methods for reading the current state of input pins. These traits are implemented by hardware abstraction layers (HALs) for specific microcontroller families, allowing developers to write portable code that works across different platforms.

```rust
use embedded_hal::digital::v2::{InputPin, OutputPin};
fn toggle_led<T: OutputPin>(led: &mut T) -> Result<(), T::Error> {
led.set_high()?;
// Some delay might be appropriate here
led.set_low()?;
Ok(())
}
```

```

Pin configuration involves setting various parameters that determine how the pin behaves. Most microcontrollers support different input and output modes, such as push-pull or open-drain outputs, and pull-up or pull-down resistors for inputs. Rust's type system can enforce correct configuration options at compile time, preventing invalid combinations that could damage hardware or cause undefined behavior.

Many microcontrollers organize their GPIO pins into ports, with each port controlling multiple pins. Rust's abstractions can represent this hardware organization while providing safe access to individual pins. The type system ensures that pins can't be simultaneously accessed from different parts of the program, preventing race conditions in concurrent applications.

Error handling in GPIO operations requires careful consideration. While basic pin operations might seem straightforward, various error conditions can occur, such as voltage violations or current overload. Rust's Result type provides a natural way to handle these errors, allowing applications to respond appropriately to hardware issues.

GPIO interrupts represent another crucial aspect of embedded systems programming. Pins configured as inputs can often generate interrupts on state changes, allowing the system to respond immediately to external events. Rust's interrupt handling mechanisms integrate well with GPIO functionality, providing safe access to shared resources from both main code and interrupt handlers.

One common pattern in embedded systems is debouncing input signals. Physical switches and buttons can produce multiple transitions when changing state, requiring software debouncing to provide clean input signals. Rust's strong abstraction capabilities
```

allow us to implement reusable debouncing logic while maintaining efficiency:

```rust
pub struct DebouncedInput<T: InputPin> {
pin: T,
state: bool,
last_change: u32,
debounce_time: u32,
}
impl<T: InputPin> DebouncedInput<T> {
pub fn new(pin: T, debounce_time: u32) -> Self{
DebouncedInput {
pin,
state: false,
last_change: 0,
debounce_time,
}
}
pub fn update(&mut self, current_time: u32) -> Result<bool,
T::Error> {
let raw_state = self.pin.is_high()?;
if raw_state != self.state &&
(current_time - self.last_change) >= self.debounce_time {
self.state = raw_state;
self.last_change = current_time;
}
Ok(self.state)
}
}
```

Power management considerations often involve GPIO configuration. Many microcontrollers allow pins to be configured in ways that minimize power consumption during sleep modes. Rust's abstractions can help manage these power-saving features while ensuring that pins remain in appropriate states during different power modes.

Testing GPIO code presents unique challenges in embedded development. While actual hardware testing is ultimately necessary, Rust's trait-based approach allows for effective unit testing using mock implementations. This capability enables developers to verify logic and error handling without physical hardware:

```rust
struct MockPin {
state: bool,
}
impl OutputPin for MockPin {
type Error = ();
fn set_high(&mut self) -> Result<(), Self::Error> {
self.state = true;
Ok(())
}
fn set_low(&mut self) -> Result<(), Self::Error> {
self.state = false;
Ok(())
}
}
```

Real-world applications often require more complex GPIO patterns. For example, LED matrices might require rapidly switching multiple pins in specific patterns, or motor controllers might need precise timing of multiple output signals. Rust's zero-cost abstractions allow these complex patterns to be implemented efficiently while maintaining safety and clarity.

Documentation plays a crucial role in GPIO programming, particularly when dealing with hardware-specific features. Rust's documentation tools help create clear, accessible documentation that includes both API details and important hardware considerations. This documentation becomes especially valuable when working with custom GPIO abstractions or specialized hardware configurations.

The future of GPIO programming in Rust continues to evolve with new hardware capabilities and application requirements. Emerging trends include better support for analog capabilities, improved interrupt handling patterns, and more sophisticated power management features. The Rust ecosystem's strong foundation in safety and abstraction provides an excellent platform for these developments.

Memory safety in GPIO programming extends beyond basic pin access. Many embedded systems must handle shared GPIO resources across different parts of the application, including interrupt handlers and multiple tasks in RTOS environments. Rust's ownership and borrowing rules help prevent common concurrency issues while maintaining efficient access to GPIO resources.

Through careful abstraction and type system usage, Rust provides a powerful yet safe approach to GPIO programming in embedded systems. The combination of compile-time checks, efficient runtime behavior, and clear abstraction boundaries makes it an excellent choice for developing reliable embedded applications that interact with the physical world through GPIO interfaces.

10. Understanding Interrupts and Exception Handling

Here's Chapter 10 - Understanding Interrupts and Exception Handling:

Interrupts and exception handling form a crucial part of embedded systems programming, allowing microcontrollers to respond to asynchronous events efficiently. In embedded Rust, we can leverage the language's safety features to handle interrupts reliably while maintaining the performance characteristics required for real time systems.

At their core, interrupts are hardware mechanisms that temporarily suspend normal program execution to handle high priority events. These events might include external signal changes, timer overflows, or peripheral communications. When an interrupt occurs, the processor saves its current state and jumps to a predetermined interrupt handler function. Rust's type system helps ensure that these handlers are defined correctly and interact safely with the rest of the program.

The basic structure of an interrupt handler in embedded Rust typically looks like this:

```rust
#[interrupt]
fn TIMER0() {
static mut COUNTER: u32 = 0;
*COUNTER += 1;
// Handle the interrupt
}
```

The #[interrupt] attribute tells the compiler that this function will be called by hardware rather than normal code. This enables important optimizations and ensures proper function prologue and epilogue generation. The static mut variable pattern is particularly important here, as it provides safe access to state that persists between interrupt invocations.

One of the key challenges in interrupt handling is safely sharing data between interrupt handlers and the main program. Rust's ownership system helps prevent data races by requiring explicit synchronization mechanisms. The cortex_m crate provides special types like Mutex that are designed for this purpose:

```rust
static SHARED_DATA: Mutex<RefCell<u32>> = Mutex::new(RefCell::new(0));
#[interrupt]
fn TIMER0() {
cortex_m::interrupt::free(|cs| {
let mut data = SHARED_DATA.borrow(cs).borrow_mut();
*data += 1;
});
}
```

Exception handling in embedded systems goes beyond just interrupts. Exceptions include events like hard faults, bus faults, and usage faults that indicate serious system problems. Rust's exception handling mechanisms allow us to recover gracefully from these conditions when possible and provide diagnostic information when recovery isn't possible.

Priority management is another crucial aspect of interrupt handling. Most microcontrollers support multiple interrupt priority levels, allowing more urgent interrupts to preempt less urgent ones. Rust's type system can help enforce correct priority assignments and prevent priority inversion problems:

```rust
```

```
unsafe {
NVIC::set_priority(Interrupt::TIMER0, Priority::P3);
NVIC::enable(Interrupt::TIMER0);
}
```

Nested interrupts present particular challenges for safety and correctness. When higher priority interrupts can preempt lower priority ones, careful attention must be paid to shared resource access and execution time constraints. Rust's static guarantees help manage this complexity by ensuring that critical sections are properly maintained and resources are accessed safely.

Real time constraints often require careful control over interrupt latency. Rust's zero cost abstractions ensure that interrupt handlers can be as efficient as hand written assembly while maintaining safety guarantees. This includes proper handling of critical sections, where interrupts must be temporarily disabled to protect shared resources:

```rust
critical_section::with(|_cs| {
// Code here runs with interrupts disabled
// Keep this section as short as possible
});
```

Error handling within interrupt contexts requires special consideration. Since panics in interrupt handlers can lead to undefined behavior, it's crucial to handle errors gracefully. Rust's Result type provides a natural way to propagate errors, but care must be taken to ensure error handling code meets real time constraints.

Debugging interrupt related issues can be challenging, but Rust provides several tools to help. The cortex_m_semihosting crate allows debug output from interrupt handlers, while the probe_run utility enables sophisticated debugging of interrupt behavior.

Additionally, Rust's strong type system often catches potential issues at compile time rather than runtime.

Resource management in interrupt handlers requires careful consideration. Since interrupt handlers run in a restricted context, they cannot allocate memory dynamically or perform certain system calls. Rust's compile time checking helps ensure that interrupt handlers only use allowed operations, preventing runtime failures.

Testing interrupt handlers presents unique challenges. While actual hardware testing is essential, Rust's abstraction capabilities allow for effective unit testing of interrupt logic. Mock objects can simulate interrupt conditions, allowing developers to verify handler behavior without physical hardware:

```rust
#[cfg(test)]
mod tests {
use super::*;
#[test]
fn test_interrupt_handler() {
let mut mock_peripheral = MockPeripheral::new();
// Simulate interrupt conditions
assert!(handle_interrupt(&mut mock_peripheral));
}
}
```

Documentation of interrupt handling code is particularly important, as it often involves hardware specific details and timing requirements. Rust's documentation tools help create clear, accessible documentation that includes both API details and important considerations for interrupt handler implementation.

Power management interactions with interrupts require careful handling. Many embedded systems use interrupts to wake from low power states, and the interrupt handling system must be configured to support this while maintaining power efficiency. Rust's type system can help ensure that power management states are correctly maintained across interrupt boundaries.

As embedded systems become more complex, interrupt handling patterns continue to evolve. Modern microcontrollers often include sophisticated interrupt controllers with features like priority inheritance and vectored interrupts. Rust's strong type system and abstraction capabilities provide an excellent foundation for implementing these advanced features while maintaining safety and performance.

Through careful use of Rust's safety features and zero cost abstractions, developers can create reliable and efficient interrupt handling systems. The combination of compile time checks, efficient runtime behavior, and clear abstraction boundaries makes Rust an excellent choice for implementing interrupt driven embedded systems that must meet strict reliability and performance requirements.

11. Timer and PWM Control

Chapter 11 focuses on Timer and PWM Control in embedded Rust applications.

Timers and Pulse Width Modulation (PWM) are fundamental components in embedded systems, enabling precise timing control and variable power output for applications ranging from motor control to LED dimming. In embedded Rust, we can leverage hardware timer peripherals and PWM modules while maintaining the language's safety guarantees.

Timer peripherals in microcontrollers serve multiple purposes. They can measure time intervals, generate periodic interrupts, trigger events, and provide the basis for PWM signal generation. Most microcontrollers feature multiple timer modules, each with configurable prescalers and counting modes. In Rust, we typically access these through Hardware Abstraction Layer (HAL) implementations that provide safe abstractions over the raw hardware.

Let's start with a basic timer configuration example. Most embedded HALs provide timer traits that abstract common functionality:

```rust
use embedded_hal::timer::CountDown;
let mut timer = dp.TIMER0.into_count_down();
timer.start(1000.milliseconds());
while !timer.wait().is_ok() {
// Timer hasn't expired yet
}
```

This pattern allows for precise timing control while preventing common errors like overflow conditions or incorrect prescaler settings. The type system ensures that timer configurations remain valid throughout the program's execution.

PWM control builds upon timer functionality to generate variable duty cycle signals. PWM is essentially a digital approximation of an analog signal, achieved by rapidly switching a digital output between high and low states. The ratio of high time to the total period (duty cycle) determines the average power delivered to the load.

A typical PWM configuration in embedded Rust might look like this:

```rust
let pwm = dp.PWM0.into_pwm();
let mut channel = pwm.get_channel(Channel::C0);
channel.set_duty(128); // 50% duty cycle for 8-bit resolution
channel.enable();
```

One of the key advantages of Rust in PWM control is the ability to create safe abstractions that prevent common errors. For example, the type system can enforce that duty cycle values remain within valid ranges and that PWM channels are properly initialized before use.

Timer accuracy is crucial in many applications. Rust's zero cost abstractions allow us to implement precise timing without runtime overhead. Consider this example of a high precision delay implementation:

```rust
pub fn precise_delay<T: CountDown>(timer: &mut T, duration: T::Time) {
timer.start(duration);
while timer.wait().is_err() {
cortex_m::asm::nop();
}
```

```
}
```

PWM frequency selection often requires careful consideration of the timer's clock source and prescaler settings. Rust's type system can help ensure that these calculations are correct at compile time:

```rust
let system_clock = 48_000_000u32; // 48 MHz
let desired_frequency = 20_000u32; // 20 kHz
let prescaler = (system_clock / desired_frequency) - 1;
pwm.set_prescaler(prescaler as u16);
```

Multiple PWM channels often need to be coordinated for applications like RGB LED control or three phase motor driving. Rust's ownership system helps prevent conflicts when managing multiple channels:

```rust
let mut red = pwm.get_channel(Channel::C0);
let mut green = pwm.get_channel(Channel::C1);
let mut blue = pwm.get_channel(Channel::C2);
// Type system ensures no channel is used twice
red.set_duty(red_value);
green.set_duty(green_value);
blue.set_duty(blue_value);
```

Timer interrupts are commonly used to implement periodic tasks. Rust's interrupt handling mechanisms integrate seamlessly with timer peripherals:

```rust
#[interrupt]
fn TIMER0() {
static mut COUNTER: u32 = 0;
*COUNTER += 1;
```

```
if *COUNTER >= PERIOD {
// Perform periodic task
*COUNTER = 0;
}
}
```

Advanced PWM features like dead time insertion for motor control applications can be safely implemented using Rust's abstractions:

```rust
pub struct MotorPWM {
pwm_high: PWMChannel,
pwm_low: PWMChannel,
dead_time: u32,
}
impl MotorPWM {
pub fn set_duty(&mut self, duty: u16) {
self.pwm_high.set_duty(duty);
self.pwm_low.set_duty(duty);
// Dead time insertion handled automatically
}
}
```

Power management considerations often involve careful timer configuration. Many microcontrollers can use timer events to wake from sleep modes:

```rust
fn enter_sleep_mode(timer: &mut Timer) {
timer.start(wake_interval);
cortex_m::asm::wfi(); // Wait for interrupt
}
```

Error handling in timer and PWM operations requires careful consideration. While many operations are guaranteed safe by the type system, some error conditions must be handled at runtime:

```rust
match pwm.set_frequency(desired_freq) {
Ok(_) => {
// Frequency set successfully
}
Err(Error::FrequencyTooHigh) => {
// Handle error condition
}
}
```

Testing timer and PWM code often requires simulation or mock implementations. Rust's trait system makes it easy to create testable abstractions:

```rust
#[cfg(test)]
mod tests {
use super::*;
struct MockTimer {
expired: bool,
}
impl CountDown for MockTimer {
type Time = u32;
fn start(&mut self, count: Self::Time) {
self.expired = false;
}
fn wait(&mut self) -> nb::Result<(), void::Void> {
if self.expired {
Ok(())
} else {
```

```
Err(nb::Error::WouldBlock)
}
}
}
}
```

Documentation of timer and PWM configurations is crucial for maintainability. Rust's documentation tools help create clear, accessible documentation that includes both API details and important considerations for implementation:

```rust
/// Configure PWM with dead time insertion for half bridge driving
///
/// # Arguments
/// * `frequency` - PWM frequency in Hz
/// * `dead_time` - Dead time in system clock cycles
///
/// # Safety
/// Ensure frequency and dead time values are within hardware limits
pub fn configure_half_bridge(frequency: u32, dead_time: u32) -> Result<HalfBridge, Error> {
// Implementation
}
```

Through careful use of Rust's safety features and zero cost abstractions, developers can create reliable and efficient timer and PWM control systems. The combination of compile time checks, efficient runtime behavior, and clear abstraction boundaries makes Rust an excellent choice for implementing precise timing and power control in embedded systems.

12. Serial Communication Protocols (UART)

Serial communication through UART (Universal Asynchronous Receiver Transmitter) is a fundamental protocol in embedded systems, enabling devices to communicate with each other and with host computers. In embedded Rust, we can implement UART communication while maintaining strong safety guarantees and efficient performance characteristics.

UART communication operates by transmitting data serially, one bit at a time, using two main signal lines: TX (transmit) and RX (receive). The protocol is asynchronous, meaning that the sender and receiver must agree on a specific baud rate beforehand, but no separate clock signal is required. This makes UART particularly useful for simple point to point communication in embedded systems.

Let's begin with a basic UART configuration in embedded Rust. Most microcontroller HALs provide UART traits that abstract the underlying hardware:

```rust
use embedded_hal::serial::{Read, Write};
let uart = dp.UART0.into_uart(
tx_pin,
rx_pin,
Config::default()
.baudrate(115200.bps())
.parity_none()
.stopbits(StopBits::STOP1)
);
```

One of Rust's key strengths in UART implementation is its ability to prevent common errors through the type system. For example, the ownership system ensures that UART pins cannot be accidentally used for other purposes while the UART peripheral is active:

```rust
let (mut tx, mut rx) = uart.split();
// tx_pin and rx_pin are now consumed and cannot be used elsewhere
```

Buffer management is crucial in UART communication. Rust's safety features help prevent buffer overruns and other common issues. Here's an example of a safe circular buffer implementation for UART reception:

```rust
pub struct UartBuffer<const N: usize> {
buffer: [u8; N],
write_index: usize,
read_index: usize,
}
impl<const N: usize> UartBuffer<N> {
pub fn push(&mut self, byte: u8) -> Result<(), BufferFullError>
{
let next_write = (self.write_index + 1) % N;
if next_write != self.read_index {
self.buffer[self.write_index] = byte;
self.write_index = next_write;
Ok(())
} else {
Err(BufferFullError)
}
}
```

```
}
```

Interrupt driven UART communication is common in embedded systems to avoid polling. Rust's interrupt handling mechanisms integrate well with UART peripherals:

```rust
#[interrupt]
fn UART0() {
static mut BUFFER: Option<UartBuffer<64>> = None;
if let Some(buffer) = BUFFER {
while let Ok(byte) = rx.read() {
if buffer.push(byte).is_err() {
// Handle buffer full condition
}
}
}
}
```

Error handling in UART communication requires careful consideration. Rust's Result type provides a clean way to handle various UART errors:

```rust
pub enum UartError {
Overrun,
Framing,
Parity,
BufferFull,
}
fn process_uart_data(uart: &mut impl Read<u8>) ->
Result<(), UartError> {
match uart.read() {
Ok(byte) => {
```

```
// Process received byte
Ok(())
}
Err(nb::Error::WouldBlock) => Ok(()),
Err(nb::Error::Other(e)) => Err(e),
}
}
```

Protocol parsing often requires state machines. Rust's enum types are particularly well suited for implementing state machines for UART protocol handling:

```rust
enum ProtocolState {
WaitingForStart,
ReadingLength(u8),
ReadingPayload(Vec<u8>, usize),
ProcessingChecksum(Vec<u8>),
}
impl ProtocolState {
fn process_byte(self, byte: u8) -> ProtocolState {
match self {
ProtocolState::WaitingForStart => {
if byte == START_BYTE {
ProtocolState::ReadingLength(0)
} else {
ProtocolState::WaitingForStart
}
}
// Additional state handling...
}
}
}
```

DMA (Direct Memory Access) is often used with UART for efficient data transfer. Rust's ownership system helps ensure safe DMA buffer management:

```rust
pub struct DmaBuffer {
buffer: &'static mut [u8],
length: usize,
}
impl DmaBuffer {
pub fn new(buffer: &'static mut [u8]) -> Self {
DmaBuffer {
buffer,
length: 0,
}
}
pub fn start_transfer(&mut self, uart: &mut Uart) {
uart.start_dma_transfer(self.buffer);
}
}
```

Testing UART implementations often requires mock objects. Rust's trait system makes it easy to create testable UART abstractions:

```rust
#[cfg(test)]
mod tests {
struct MockUart {
tx_buffer: Vec<u8>,
rx_buffer: Vec<u8>,
}
impl Read<u8> for MockUart {
```

```
type Error = void::Void;
fn read(&mut self) -> nb::Result<u8, Self::Error> {
if let Some(byte) = self.rx_buffer.pop() {
Ok(byte)
} else {
Err(nb::Error::WouldBlock)
}
}
}
}
```

Power management considerations often involve UART configuration. Many systems need to disable UART peripherals to save power:

```rust
impl UartManager {
pub fn enter_low_power(&mut self) {
self.uart.disable();
self.tx_pin.into_floating_input();
self.rx_pin.into_floating_input();
}
pub fn exit_low_power(&mut self) {
self.uart.enable();
// Reconfigure pins and UART
}
}
```

Documentation for UART implementations should include clear information about timing requirements and configuration options:

```rust
/// Configure UART with specified parameters
```

```
///
/// # Arguments
/// * `baudrate` - Communication speed in bits per second
/// * `config` - Additional configuration options
///
/// # Notes
/// Ensure system clock is properly configured for desired baudrate
pub fn configure_uart(
baudrate: u32,
config: UartConfig,
) -> Result<Uart, UartError> {
// Implementation
}
```

Through careful application of Rust's safety features and zero cost abstractions, developers can create reliable and efficient UART communication systems. The combination of compile time checks, efficient runtime behavior, and clear abstraction boundaries makes Rust an excellent choice for implementing serial communication in embedded systems.

13. I2C Protocol Implementation

The Inter-Integrated Circuit (I2C) protocol stands as one of the most widely used communication protocols in embedded systems, offering a robust and versatile solution for device-to-device communication. For embedded Rust developers, understanding and implementing I2C communication effectively is crucial for building reliable systems. This chapter explores the intricacies of I2C implementation while leveraging Rust's powerful safety features and performance capabilities.

At its core, I2C operates using two signal lines: Serial Data (SDA) and Serial Clock (SCL). This seemingly simple two-wire interface belies the protocol's sophistication and flexibility. The beauty of I2C lies in its support for multiple masters and multiple slaves on the same bus, making it ideal for complex embedded systems where numerous peripherals need to communicate with one another. Each slave device on the bus has a unique address, typically 7 bits long (though 10-bit addressing is also supported), allowing for efficient communication between multiple devices while maintaining signal integrity.

When implementing I2C in Rust, we leverage the embedded-hal traits to ensure our code remains portable across different microcontroller platforms. The embedded-hal crate provides standardized traits for I2C communication, allowing us to write platform-agnostic code that can be easily ported to different hardware. These traits include basic read and write operations, as well as more complex combined operations like write-read sequences that are commonly needed when communicating with I2C peripherals.

Error handling plays a crucial role in robust I2C implementations. Common issues include bus errors, device timeout, addressing problems, and arbitration losses in multi-master setups. Rust's type system helps us handle these errors gracefully through the Result type and custom error enums. This approach ensures that error conditions are handled explicitly, preventing silent failures that could compromise system reliability.

One of the key considerations when implementing I2C communication is timing. The protocol supports different speed modes, including Standard Mode (100 kHz), Fast Mode (400 kHz), and Fast Mode Plus (1 MHz). The choice of speed mode depends on various factors including the capabilities of both master and slave devices, bus capacitance, and system requirements. Rust's zero-cost abstractions allow us to implement timing-critical code without runtime overhead, ensuring reliable communication even at higher speeds.

Clock stretching is another important aspect of I2C communication that requires careful consideration in our implementation. This mechanism allows slave devices to temporarily hold the clock line low, essentially pausing communication when they need more time to process data or prepare a response. Our Rust implementation must properly handle clock stretching to ensure reliable communication with slower devices while maintaining system responsiveness.

The concept of arbitration becomes crucial in multi-master systems. When multiple masters attempt to initiate communication simultaneously, the I2C protocol includes built-in arbitration that allows the highest priority master (determined by the message address bits) to gain control of the bus while other masters automatically back off. Implementing this behavior correctly in Rust requires careful attention to the protocol timing and state management.

For practical applications, we often need to implement higher-level abstractions on top of the basic I2C communication layer. This might include device-specific drivers for sensors, displays, or other peripherals. Rust's trait system allows us to create clean, reusable abstractions that encapsulate device-specific behavior while maintaining type safety and zero-cost abstractions.

When working with I2C in resource-constrained environments, optimization becomes crucial. Rust's zero-cost abstractions shine here, allowing us to write high-level, safe code that compiles down to efficient machine code. Techniques like static dispatch and const generics can be used to eliminate runtime overhead while maintaining code clarity and safety.

Testing I2C implementations presents unique challenges in embedded systems. We'll explore strategies for unit testing I2C code using mock implementations of the embedded-hal traits, as well as integration testing approaches using real hardware. Rust's powerful type system and testing framework help ensure our I2C implementation remains reliable across different scenarios and edge cases.

Throughout this chapter, we've emphasized the importance of balancing safety, performance, and maintainability in I2C implementations. Rust's unique features make it particularly well-suited for this task, allowing us to write code that is both safe and efficient. As we move forward with more complex embedded systems, having a solid understanding of I2C implementation in Rust will prove invaluable for building reliable and performant applications.

14. SPI Communication

The Serial Peripheral Interface (SPI) protocol stands as one of the most widely used communication standards in embedded systems, offering high speed data transfer with a simple yet effective synchronous protocol. In embedded Rust development, working with SPI requires understanding both the hardware fundamentals and the software abstractions that make it reliable and efficient. This chapter explores the implementation of SPI communication using Rust, covering everything from basic concepts to advanced usage patterns.

SPI communication operates on a master slave architecture, where one device (typically the microcontroller) acts as the master, controlling the clock signal and coordinating data transfer with one or more slave devices. The protocol uses four primary signals: SCLK (Serial Clock), MOSI (Master Out Slave In), MISO (Master In Slave Out), and CS/SS (Chip Select/Slave Select). This configuration allows for full duplex communication, meaning data can be sent and received simultaneously.

In embedded Rust, SPI communication is typically implemented through the embedded hal traits, which provide a standardized interface for working with SPI peripherals across different microcontroller platforms. The primary traits involved are SpiDevice and SpiBus, which encapsulate the core functionality needed for SPI communication. Let's examine a basic implementation of SPI communication in Rust:

```rust
use embedded_hal::spi::{Mode, Phase, Polarity};
use embedded_hal::digital::v2::OutputPin;
pub struct SpiDevice<SPI, CS> {
spi: SPI,
cs: CS,
```

```
}
impl<SPI, CS> SpiDevice<SPI, CS>
where
SPI: embedded_hal::spi::FullDuplex<u8>,
CS: OutputPin,
{
pub fn new(spi: SPI, cs: CS) -> Self {
Self { spi, cs }
}
pub fn transfer(&mut self, data: &[u8]) -> Result<Vec<u8>,
Error> {
self.cs.set_low().map_err(Error::Cs)?;
let mut result = Vec::with_capacity(data.len());
for byte in data {
self.spi.send(*byte).map_err(Error::Spi)?;
let received = self.spi.read().map_err(Error::Spi)?;
result.push(received);
}
self.cs.set_high().map_err(Error::Cs)?;
Ok(result)
}
}
```

One of the key considerations when working with SPI in embedded Rust is the configuration of the SPI mode. SPI modes are defined by the combination of clock polarity (CPOL) and clock phase (CPHA), resulting in four possible modes (0 through 3). The correct mode must be selected based on the requirements of the slave device being communicated with. Rust's type system helps ensure that these configurations are correctly specified at compile time:

```rust
let mode = Mode {
```

```
polarity: Polarity::IdleLow,
phase: Phase::CaptureOnFirstTransition,
};
```

When working with multiple slave devices on a single SPI bus, proper management of chip select signals becomes crucial. Rust's ownership and borrowing rules help prevent common errors such as accidentally enabling multiple slave devices simultaneously or forgetting to disable a device after communication. Here's an example of how to implement a multi device SPI manager:

```rust
pub struct SpiManager<SPI> {
spi: SPI,
devices: Vec<(Pin, DeviceConfig)>,
}
impl<SPI> SpiManager<SPI>
where
SPI: embedded_hal::spi::FullDuplex<u8>,
{
pub fn communicate_with_device(&mut self, device_id: usize, data: &[u8]) -> Result<Vec<u8>, Error> {
if let Some((cs_pin, config)) = self.devices.get_mut(device_id) {
cs_pin.set_low().map_err(Error::Cs)?;
// Configure SPI parameters for this specific device
self.configure_spi(config)?;
let result = self.transfer(data)?;
cs_pin.set_high().map_err(Error::Cs)?;
Ok(result)
} else {
Err(Error::InvalidDevice)
}
}
```

```
}
```

Error handling is particularly important in SPI communication, as various issues can arise during data transfer. Rust's Result type provides a clean way to handle and propagate errors through the application. Common error cases include communication timeouts, invalid data formats, and chip select failures. Here's an example of a comprehensive error type for SPI operations:

```rust
#[derive(Debug)]
pub enum SpiError {
TransferError,
ConfigurationError,
ChipSelectError,
TimeoutError,
BufferOverflow,
InvalidData,
}
```

Performance optimization is another crucial aspect of SPI communication in embedded systems. Rust's zero cost abstractions allow for efficient implementations without sacrificing safety or readability. DMA (Direct Memory Access) can be used for larger data transfers, and careful buffer management can help minimize memory usage:

```rust
pub struct DmaSpiTransfer<SPI, DMA> {
spi: SPI,
dma: DMA,
buffer: &'static mut [u8],
}
impl<SPI, DMA> DmaSpiTransfer<SPI, DMA>
```

```
where
SPI: embedded_hal::spi::FullDuplex<u8>,
DMA: embedded_hal::blocking::dma::Transfer<W>,
{
pub fn transfer_dma(&mut self, data: &[u8]) -> Result<(), Error> {
self.dma.start(data, self.buffer)?;
while !self.dma.is_done() {
continue;
}
Ok(())
}
}
```

Testing SPI implementations requires careful consideration of hardware dependencies. Rust's powerful testing framework can be used to create mock implementations for testing communication logic without actual hardware:

```rust
#[cfg(test)]
mod tests {
use super::*;
struct MockSpi {
expected_data: Vec<u8>,
response_data: Vec<u8>,
}
impl embedded_hal::spi::FullDuplex<u8> for MockSpi {
type Error = ();
fn send(&mut self, byte: u8) -> Result<(), Self::Error> {
assert_eq!(byte, self.expected_data.remove(0));
Ok(())
}
```

```
fn read(&mut self) -> Result<u8, Self::Error> {
Ok(self.response_data.remove(0))
}
}
}
```

The chapter concludes by emphasizing the importance of proper documentation and error handling in SPI implementations. When working with embedded systems, robust error handling and clear documentation can save countless hours of debugging and maintenance work. The combination of Rust's safety features and the embedded hal abstractions provides a solid foundation for building reliable SPI communication in embedded systems.

15. Memory Management in Embedded Rust

Memory management in embedded Rust represents one of the most critical aspects of developing reliable and efficient embedded systems. Unlike general purpose computing environments, embedded systems often operate with severe memory constraints and lack traditional memory management facilities like virtual memory or garbage collection. This chapter explores how Rust's ownership model and zero cost abstractions enable precise control over memory usage while maintaining safety guarantees.

In embedded systems, memory is typically divided into several distinct regions: Flash memory for program storage, RAM for runtime data, and potentially EEPROM or other non volatile storage for persistent data. Rust's compile time checks ensure that code respects these boundaries while preventing common memory related bugs like buffer overflows, use after free errors, and data races.

The static memory model in embedded Rust begins with the linker script, which defines how different memory sections are organized. A typical embedded Rust program might include sections for code (.text), initialized data (.data), uninitialized data (.bss), and stack space. Here's how you might define memory regions in a linker script:

```rust
MEMORY
{
FLASH : ORIGIN = 0x08000000, LENGTH = 64K
RAM : ORIGIN = 0x20000000, LENGTH = 20K
}
```

One of the most powerful features of Rust for embedded memory management is the ability to statically allocate resources. The static keyword allows developers to create globals that are initialized at compile time and guaranteed to exist throughout the program's lifetime. However, static mut variables require unsafe blocks to access, encouraging careful consideration of shared mutable state:

```rust
static mut GLOBAL_BUFFER: [u8; 1024] = [0; 1024];
fn process_data() {
unsafe {
GLOBAL_BUFFER[0] = 42;
}
}
```

Heap allocation in embedded systems presents unique challenges. Many embedded systems operate without a heap altogether, relying solely on stack allocation and static memory. However, when dynamic allocation is necessary, Rust provides several options. The alloc crate can be used with a custom allocator tailored to embedded constraints:

```rust
use linked_list_allocator::LinkedListAllocator;
#[global_allocator]
static ALLOCATOR: LinkedListAllocator = LinkedListAllocator::new();
#[no_mangle]
unsafe fn initialize_heap() {
const HEAP_SIZE: usize = 1024;
static mut HEAP: [u8; HEAP_SIZE] = [0; HEAP_SIZE];
ALLOCATOR.init(HEAP.as_ptr() as usize, HEAP_SIZE);
}
```

For systems that require more fine grained control over memory allocation, Rust provides the allocator_api feature. This allows implementation of custom allocators that can be used with standard collection types:

```rust
pub struct BumpAllocator {
heap_start: usize,
heap_end: usize,
next: usize,
}
unsafe impl GlobalAlloc for BumpAllocator {
unsafe fn alloc(&self, layout: Layout) -> *mut u8 {
let size = layout.size();
let align = layout.align();
let aligned_next = align_up(self.next, align);
if aligned_next + size > self.heap_end {
null_mut()
} else {
self.next = aligned_next + size;
aligned_next as *mut u8
}
}
unsafe fn dealloc(&self, _ptr: *mut u8, _layout: Layout) {
// This simple allocator doesn't support deallocation
}
}
```

Stack usage requires careful consideration in embedded systems. Rust's ownership model helps prevent stack overflow by making stack usage explicit and analyzable at compile time. The #[inline]

and #[inline(never)] attributes can be used to control function inlining, affecting both performance and stack usage:

```rust
#[inline(never)]
fn large_stack_function() {
let buffer = [0u8; 1024];
process_buffer(&buffer);
}
```

Memory fragmentation can be a serious issue in long running embedded systems. Rust's compile time guarantees help prevent fragmentation by encouraging the use of fixed size allocations and stack based processing. When dynamic allocation is necessary, arena allocators can be used to manage memory in a more predictable way:

```rust
use typed_arena::Arena;
struct ArenaManager<'a> {
string_arena: Arena<String>,
buffer_arena: Arena<Vec<u8>>,
lifetime: PhantomData<&'a ()>,
}
impl<'a> ArenaManager<'a> {
pub fn new() -> Self {
Self {
string_arena: Arena::new(),
buffer_arena: Arena::new(),
lifetime: PhantomData,
}
}
pub fn allocate_string(&self, content: &str) -> &String {
self.string_arena.alloc(content.to_string())
}
```

```
}
```

Error handling in memory constrained environments requires special consideration. Rather than using Result types that might allocate, embedded Rust code often uses statically sized error handling mechanisms:

```rust
#[derive(Debug)]
pub enum MemoryError {
OutOfMemory,
AlignmentError,
AddressOutOfRange,
}
type MemoryResult<T> = Result<T, MemoryError>;
```

Memory safety in interrupt handlers presents unique challenges. Rust's ownership system helps ensure that shared resources are accessed safely, even in interrupt contexts:

```rust
static SHARED_BUFFER: Mutex<RefCell<[u8; 1024]>> = Mutex::new(RefCell::new([0; 1024]));
#[interrupt]
fn UART0() {
cortex_m::interrupt::free(|cs| {
if let Some(buffer) = SHARED_BUFFER.borrow(cs).borrow_mut().get_mut(0) {
*buffer = read_uart();
}
});
}
```

The chapter concludes by emphasizing the importance of careful memory management in embedded systems. Rust's ownership model, combined with its powerful type system and zero cost abstractions, provides the tools necessary to build memory safe and efficient embedded applications. By understanding these concepts and applying them appropriately, developers can create robust embedded systems that make the most of limited resources while maintaining high reliability standards.

16. Zero-Cost Abstractions Explained

Zero-cost abstractions represent one of Rust's most powerful features, especially in the context of embedded systems where resource efficiency is paramount. These abstractions allow developers to write high-level, expressive code without incurring runtime overhead, making them particularly valuable for resource-constrained environments.

At its core, a zero-cost abstraction means that using the abstraction results in machine code that is just as efficient as if you had written the low-level code by hand. This concept, originally popularized in C++, has been embraced and enhanced by Rust's design philosophy. The key principle is that you pay for only what you use, and abstractions compile down to the same code you would have written directly.

Consider iterators, one of Rust's most commonly used zero-cost abstractions. When you write high-level iterator chains, the compiler optimizes them into efficient machine code:

```rust
let buffer = [1, 2, 3, 4, 5];
let sum: u32 = buffer.iter()
.filter(|&&x| x % 2 == 0)
.map(|&x| x * x)
.sum();
```

This code looks like it might create intermediate collections and require multiple passes over the data. However, the compiler optimizes this into essentially a single loop with direct arithmetic operations, equivalent to writing the low-level implementation manually.

Generics provide another powerful example of zero cost abstractions in Rust. Through monomorphization, the compiler generates specialized versions of generic functions for each concrete type they're used with. This means generic code runs just as fast as type-specific implementations:

```rust
struct Buffer<T> {
data: [T; 64],
position: usize,
}
impl<T> Buffer<T> {
pub fn push(&mut self, item: T) -> Result<(), ()> {
if self.position < self.data.len() {
self.data[self.position] = item;
self.position += 1;
Ok(())
} else {
Err(())
}
}
}
```

When this generic buffer is used with specific types, the compiler generates separate, optimized implementations for each type, eliminating any runtime overhead from the generic abstraction.

Traits in Rust also demonstrate zero-cost abstraction principles. Static dispatch through trait bounds allows the compiler to resolve trait method calls at compile time, avoiding the overhead of virtual dispatch:

```rust
trait Peripheral {
fn initialize(&mut self);
fn write(&mut self, data: u8);
fn read(&mut self) -> u8;
```

```
}
fn configure_peripheral<T: Peripheral>(device: &mut T) {
device.initialize();
}
```

The compiler generates specific implementations for each type that implements Peripheral, eliminating any runtime cost for trait method dispatch.

Another powerful zero-cost abstraction in Rust is the type state pattern, which enables compile-time state machine verification without runtime overhead:

```rust
struct Uninitialized;
struct Initialized;
struct PeripheralDevice<State> {
address: u32,
_state: PhantomData<State>,
}
impl PeripheralDevice<Uninitialized> {
pub fn new(address: u32) -> Self {
PeripheralDevice {
address,
_state: PhantomData,
}
}
pub fn initialize(self) -> PeripheralDevice<Initialized> {
// Perform initialization
PeripheralDevice {
address: self.address,
_state: PhantomData,
}
}
```

```rust
}
impl PeripheralDevice<Initialized> {
pub fn write(&mut self, data: u8) {
// Safe to write only after initialization
unsafe {
write_volatile(self.address as *mut u8, data);
}
}
}
```

This pattern provides compile-time guarantees about state transitions without adding any runtime overhead.

Resource management in Rust, including RAII (Resource Acquisition Is Initialization), represents another zero-cost abstraction. The compiler ensures proper resource cleanup without runtime overhead:

```rust
struct SpiTransaction<'a> {
spi: &'a mut Spi,
}
impl<'a> SpiTransaction <'a> {
fn new(spi: &'a mut Spi) -> Self {
spi.chip_select_low();
SpiTransaction { spi }
}
}
impl<'a> Drop for SpiTransaction<'a> {
fn drop(&mut self) {
self.spi.chip_select_high();
}
}
```

The Drop trait implementation ensures cleanup code runs at compile-time determined points, with no runtime tracking overhead.

Embedded systems often require bit-level operations, and Rust provides zero-cost abstractions for these through its bitfield implementations:

```rust
#[repr(C)]
struct RegisterBlock {
control: u32,
status: u32,
}
impl RegisterBlock {
#[inline]
pub fn set_enable(&mut self) {
self.control |= 1 << 0;
}
#[inline]
pub fn is_busy(&self) -> bool {
(self.status & (1 << 1)) != 0
}
}
```

These methods compile to direct bit manipulation instructions, with no additional overhead compared to manual bit operations.

The compiler's ability to optimize away bounds checks in proven-safe contexts is another example of zero-cost abstractions:

```rust
fn process_fixed_buffer(buffer: &[u8; 16]) {
for i in 0..16 {
// No runtime bounds check needed
let byte = buffer[i];
```

```
process_byte(byte);
}
}
```

When the compiler can prove that array access is within bounds, it eliminates the runtime checks while maintaining safety guarantees.

Understanding and leveraging zero-cost abstractions is crucial for embedded Rust development. They enable developers to write clear, maintainable code while achieving performance equivalent to hand-optimized low-level implementations. This combination of safety, expressiveness, and efficiency makes Rust particularly well-suited for embedded systems development.

17. Working with Arduino in Rust

Working with Arduino in Rust opens up exciting possibilities for embedded development by combining the safety and expressiveness of Rust with Arduino's widespread accessibility and extensive hardware ecosystem. While Arduino traditionally uses C++, Rust provides a more robust alternative that maintains performance while adding memory safety guarantees.

The Arduino ecosystem can be accessed through Rust using the arduino hal crate, which provides a hardware abstraction layer specifically designed for Arduino boards. This allows developers to write Rust code that directly interfaces with Arduino hardware while maintaining Rust's safety guarantees.

To begin working with Arduino in Rust, you'll first need to install the appropriate toolchain. This includes the avr gcc toolchain for AVR based Arduino boards or the arm none eabi gcc toolchain for ARM based boards like the Arduino Due. The installation process varies by operating system, but package managers like apt on Linux or Homebrew on macOS typically provide these tools.

The basic structure of an Arduino program in Rust differs from traditional Arduino sketches. Instead of the familiar setup() and loop() functions, Rust programs use a main() function that contains the program's entry point. Here's a basic example that demonstrates the classic LED blink program:

```rust
#![no_std]
#![no_main]
use arduino_hal::prelude::*;
use panic_halt as _;
#[arduino_hal::entry]
fn main() -> ! {
let dp = arduino_hal::Peripherals::take().unwrap();
```

```
let pins = arduino_hal::pins!(dp);
let mut led = pins.d13.into_output();
loop {
led.toggle();
arduino_hal::delay_ms(1000);
}
}
```

This example demonstrates several key concepts of Arduino programming in Rust. The #![no_std] attribute indicates that we're not using the standard library, as it's not available on embedded systems. The #![no_main] attribute tells the compiler that we're providing our own entry point. The panic_halt crate provides basic panic handling for when things go wrong.

One significant advantage of using Rust with Arduino is the type system's ability to prevent common errors. For example, when working with digital pins, the type system ensures you can't accidentally read from an output pin or write to an input pin:

```rust
let mut led_pin = pins.d13.into_output();
led_pin.set_high(); // This works
let value = led_pin.is_set_high(); // This works too
// This would cause a compile error:
// let input_value = led_pin.is_high(); // Error: method not available
```

Serial communication, a fundamental feature of Arduino development, is also well supported in Rust. The serial interface provides type safe methods for sending and receiving data:

```rust
let dp = arduino_hal::Peripherals::take().unwrap();
let pins = arduino_hal::pins!(dp);
```

```
let mut serial = arduino_hal::default_serial!(dp, pins, 57600);
loop {
serial.write_str("Hello from Rust!\r\n").unwrap();
arduino_hal::delay_ms(1000);
}
```

Analog input and output operations are similarly well supported, with the ADC (Analog to Digital Converter) interface providing safe access to analog readings:

```rust
let dp = arduino_hal::Peripherals::take().unwrap();
let pins = arduino_hal::pins!(dp);
let mut adc = arduino_hal::Adc::new(dp.ADC, Default::default());
let a0 = pins.a0.into_analog_input(&mut adc);
loop {
let reading: u16 = a0.analog_read(&mut adc);
// reading now contains a value between 0 and 1023
}
```

Working with timers in Rust provides more precise control than the traditional Arduino delay functions. Rust's type system ensures that timer configurations are valid at compile time:

```rust
let dp = arduino_hal::Peripherals::take().unwrap();
let tc0 = dp.TC0;
let timer = tc0.timer0(
arduino_hal::clock::Clock::new_16mhz(),
arduino_hal::time::Microseconds(1000),
);
loop {
timer.start().unwrap();
```

```
while !timer.is_done() {}
// Timer has elapsed
}
```

Interrupts can be handled safely in Rust using the avr_device crate's interrupt infrastructure. This provides a safe wrapper around hardware interrupts while maintaining Rust's ownership rules:

```rust
#[avr_device::interrupt(atmega328p)]
fn TIMER1_COMPA() {
static mut LED: Option<Pin<Output>> = None;
if let Some(led) = LED {
led.toggle();
}
}
```

One particularly powerful feature when working with Arduino in Rust is the ability to use Rust's powerful trait system to create reusable abstractions. For example, you can define traits for different types of sensors:

```rust
trait TemperatureSensor {
fn read_temperature(&mut self) -> Result<f32, ()>;
fn set_resolution(&mut self, bits: u8) -> Result<(), ()>;
}
struct Dht11<P: InputPin> {
pin: P,
}
impl<P: InputPin> TemperatureSensor for Dht11<P> {
fn read_temperature(&mut self) -> Result<f32, ()> {
// Implementation details
}
```

```
fn set_resolution(&mut self, bits: u8) -> Result<(), ()> {
// Implementation details
}
}
```

Memory safety becomes particularly important when working with Arduino's limited resources. Rust's ownership system helps prevent common issues like buffer overflows and use after free errors. For example, when working with buffers:

```rust
struct CircularBuffer<T, const N: usize> {
data: [T; N],
head: usize,
tail: usize,
}
impl<T: Default + Copy, const N: usize> CircularBuffer<T, N> {
pub fn new() -> Self {
Self {
data: [T::default(); N],
head: 0,
tail: 0,
}
}
pub fn push(&mut self, item: T) -> Result<(), ()> {
let next = (self.head + 1) % N;
if next != self.tail {
self.data[self.head] = item;
self.head = next;
Ok(())
} else {
Err(())
```

```
        }
    }
}
```

Working with Arduino in Rust provides a robust foundation for embedded development that combines the best of both worlds: Arduino's accessible hardware platform and extensive ecosystem with Rust's strong safety guarantees and modern language features. This combination enables developers to create more reliable and maintainable embedded systems while maintaining the simplicity and approachability that made Arduino popular in the first place.

18. Arduino Project: Smart Environmental Monitor

In this chapter, we'll apply our knowledge of embedded Rust to create a practical Arduino-based smart environmental monitoring system. This project serves as an excellent demonstration of how Rust's safety features and performance benefits can be leveraged in real-world embedded applications, while also introducing essential concepts in sensor integration and data management.

Our smart environmental monitor combines multiple sensors to track temperature, humidity, air quality, and light levels in real-time. This project is particularly relevant for modern IoT applications, from smart home systems to industrial environmental monitoring. By implementing this project in Rust, we'll demonstrate how to create reliable and efficient embedded systems that can run continuously for extended periods.

The heart of our environmental monitor uses the BME280 sensor for temperature, humidity, and pressure measurements, alongside an MQ-135 sensor for air quality monitoring and a photoresistor for ambient light detection. These sensors communicate with our Arduino through different protocols we've covered in previous chapters - I2C for the BME280 and analog inputs for the MQ-135 and photoresistor. This combination of sensors and protocols provides an excellent opportunity to demonstrate protocol integration in a real-world context.

Memory management becomes particularly important in this project as we handle continuous sensor readings and maintain historical data. Rust's ownership system helps us ensure that our data handling is both memory-efficient and safe. We'll implement a circular buffer to store historical sensor readings, demonstrating how Rust's safety guarantees help prevent common embedded programming pitfalls like buffer overflows.

Error handling takes center stage in this project as we deal with multiple potential points of failure - sensor communication errors, data storage issues, and system state management. We'll implement a robust error handling strategy that ensures our environmental monitor can recover gracefully from errors without requiring manual intervention. This approach showcases how Rust's Result type and error handling patterns can be effectively applied in embedded systems.

Power efficiency is crucial for an environmental monitoring system that might need to run on battery power. We'll explore techniques for optimizing power consumption, including implementing sleep modes and adjusting sensor sampling rates based on activity levels. Rust's zero-cost abstractions ensure that our power management code remains efficient while being easy to understand and maintain.

Data presentation forms an important aspect of our environmental monitor. We'll implement a simple LCD display interface to show current readings and basic statistics. For more detailed data analysis, we'll add serial communication capabilities to allow logging to a connected computer. This demonstrates how to handle multiple output interfaces while maintaining code clarity and system responsiveness.

Calibration is essential for accurate environmental monitoring. We'll implement a calibration routine for our sensors, storing calibration data in the Arduino's EEPROM. This provides an opportunity to explore persistent storage in embedded systems while ensuring our measurements remain accurate over time. Rust's type system helps us maintain the integrity of our calibration data and prevents common errors in data handling.

Real-world environmental monitoring often requires handling various measurement units and conversions. We'll use Rust's type system to create safe unit conversions and prevent common measurement errors. This approach demonstrates how Rust's strong typing can be leveraged to create more reliable embedded systems.

As our environmental monitor collects sensitive data about its environment, security considerations become important. We'll implement basic data encryption for stored readings and implement secure communication protocols for data transmission. This showcases how Rust's security features can be applied in embedded systems to protect sensitive environmental data.

Testing plays a crucial role in ensuring our environmental monitor's reliability. We'll develop a comprehensive testing strategy that includes unit tests for our sensor interfaces, integration tests for the complete system, and stress testing under various environmental conditions. Rust's testing framework makes it straightforward to implement thorough testing while maintaining code quality.

The project concludes with suggestions for potential expansions and modifications. These might include adding wireless connectivity for remote monitoring, implementing more sophisticated data analysis algorithms, or adding additional sensor types. This forward-looking approach helps readers understand how to extend and adapt the project for their specific needs.

By the end of this chapter, readers will have gained hands-on experience in building a complete embedded system in Rust, from sensor integration to data management and user interface implementation. This project serves as a template for developing other embedded monitoring systems while demonstrating the practical benefits of using Rust in embedded development.

The smart environmental monitor project exemplifies how Rust's safety features, performance capabilities, and modern development practices can be applied to create reliable and efficient embedded systems. Through this practical implementation, we've demonstrated that Rust is not just a theoretically superior choice for embedded development, but also a practical and powerful tool for real-world applications.

19. Arduino Project: Digital Control System

In this chapter, we'll develop a comprehensive digital control system using Arduino and Rust, demonstrating how to implement precise, real-time control mechanisms for physical systems. This project showcases the power of Rust in handling time-critical operations while maintaining safety and reliability in control applications.

• • • •

OUR DIGITAL CONTROL system project focuses on implementing a PID (Proportional-Integral-Derivative) controller, one of the most widely used control algorithms in industrial applications. We'll create a system that can maintain a specific setpoint by continuously adjusting its output based on feedback from sensors. This practical implementation demonstrates both the theoretical aspects of control systems and the robust capabilities of Rust in embedded applications.

• • • •

THE SYSTEM WE'LL BUILD can be configured for various applications, such as temperature control, motor speed regulation, or position control. For our specific implementation, we'll focus on motor speed control, using a DC motor with an encoder for feedback. This setup provides an excellent platform for learning about real-time control systems while dealing with practical challenges like sensor noise, system delays, and mechanical limitations.

• • • •

AT THE CORE OF OUR implementation lies the challenge of sampling and timing precision. Rust's zero-cost abstractions allow us to create highly efficient timer interrupts and precise sampling mechanisms. We'll explore how to use Arduino's hardware timers through Rust abstractions, ensuring consistent sampling intervals critical for stable control system operation. The system samples the encoder feedback at regular intervals, typically every few milliseconds, requiring careful attention to timing precision and interrupt handling.

• • • •

ERROR HANDLING BECOMES particularly crucial in control systems where system stability is paramount. We'll implement comprehensive error detection and handling mechanisms, including overflow protection for our PID calculations, sensor failure detection, and safety limits for output values. Rust's type system and error handling patterns help us create a robust system that can handle edge cases gracefully without compromising control stability.

• • • •

THE PID ALGORITHM IMPLEMENTATION showcases Rust's strength in handling floating-point calculations efficiently while preventing common numerical errors. We'll implement the controller using fixed-point arithmetic for better performance on the Arduino's limited hardware. This approach demonstrates how to balance computational efficiency with numerical accuracy, a common challenge in embedded control systems.

• • • •

TUNING A PID CONTROLLER requires careful adjustment of multiple parameters. We'll create a parameter adjustment interface that allows real-time modification of the PID constants through serial communication. This feature demonstrates how to handle dynamic parameter updates safely in a running system, showcasing Rust's strong guarantees about data consistency and thread safety even in an interrupt-driven environment.

• • • •

STATE MANAGEMENT IN our control system requires careful consideration of different operating modes - initialization, normal operation, fault conditions, and shutdown sequences. We'll implement a state machine pattern that clearly defines system behavior in each mode while ensuring safe transitions between states. Rust's enum types and pattern matching make this implementation both clear and efficient.

• • • •

DATA LOGGING CAPABILITIES are essential for analyzing control system performance. We'll implement a circular buffer to store recent system data, including setpoint, measured values, and control outputs. This data can be transmitted via serial communication for real-time monitoring and analysis. We'll show how to implement this feature efficiently while ensuring it doesn't interfere with the critical control loop timing.

• • • •

OUR SYSTEM INCLUDES various safety features crucial for real-world applications. We'll implement soft and hard limits on control outputs, rate-of-change limitations, and watchdog functionality. These features demonstrate how to create fail-safe mechanisms in Rust while maintaining system reliability and predictability.

• • • •

THE USER INTERFACE portion of our project includes both hardware interfaces (LED indicators and switches) and a serial communication protocol for configuration and monitoring. We'll create a clean API for interacting with the control system, demonstrating how to design interfaces that are both user-friendly and robust against incorrect usage.

• • • •

TESTING A CONTROL SYSTEM presents unique challenges, as it involves both software correctness and physical system behavior. We'll develop a testing strategy that includes unit tests for the control algorithm, simulation-based testing for system dynamics, and practical methods for validating system performance. This approach shows how to leverage Rust's testing framework in embedded systems context.

• • • •

MEMORY MANAGEMENT IN our control system focuses on static allocation patterns to ensure predictable behavior. We'll demonstrate how to use Rust's compile-time guarantees to prevent memory-related issues while maintaining efficient operation. This includes careful consideration of stack usage in interrupt handlers and avoiding dynamic allocation during critical control operations.

• • • •

BY THE END OF THIS chapter, readers will have a thorough understanding of implementing digital control systems using Rust on Arduino hardware. The project serves as a practical example of how Rust's safety features and performance capabilities can be applied to create reliable control systems. We'll conclude with suggestions for extending the system, such as adding network connectivity for remote monitoring or implementing more advanced control algorithms.

• • • •

OUR DIGITAL CONTROL system project demonstrates that Rust is not just suitable but excels in creating robust, efficient embedded control applications. The combination of safety guarantees, performance optimization, and clear error handling makes Rust an excellent choice for implementing critical control systems in real-world applications.

20. STM32 Platform Introduction

The STM32 family of microcontrollers represents one of the most popular and versatile platforms for embedded systems development. Based on ARM Cortex M cores, these microcontrollers offer an excellent balance of performance, power efficiency, and peripheral features that make them ideal for a wide range of applications. In this chapter, we'll explore the fundamentals of STM32 microcontrollers and prepare you for embedded Rust development on this platform.

STM32 microcontrollers are manufactured by STMicroelectronics and come in several series, each optimized for different use cases. The most commonly used series include the STM32F0 (entry level), STM32F1 (mainstream), STM32F4 (high performance), and STM32L4 (ultra low power). Each series offers different combinations of processing power, memory capacity, and peripheral features, allowing developers to choose the most appropriate chip for their specific requirements.

At the heart of most STM32 microcontrollers is an ARM Cortex M processor. The Cortex M architecture is specifically designed for embedded applications, providing an excellent foundation for real time processing and efficient interrupt handling. When programming STM32 devices with Rust, we can take full advantage of these architectural features while maintaining the safety guarantees that make Rust such an attractive choice for embedded development.

One of the key advantages of working with STM32 microcontrollers is their rich peripheral set. Most STM32 devices include multiple communication interfaces (UART, I2C, SPI), analog to digital converters (ADC), digital to analog converters (DAC), timers, and direct memory access (DMA) controllers. These peripherals are crucial for interfacing with external devices and implementing complex embedded applications. Rust's strong type system and ownership model help ensure that these peripherals are used safely and correctly.

The memory architecture of STM32 devices is particularly important to understand when developing with Rust. Most STM32 microcontrollers feature separate flash memory for program storage and SRAM for runtime data. The amount of available memory varies significantly between different models, from a few kilobytes in the smallest devices to hundreds of kilobytes in high end variants. Rust's zero cost abstractions are particularly valuable here, as they allow us to write clean, maintainable code without incurring runtime overhead that would waste precious memory resources.

For development purposes, STM32 microcontrollers typically provide a JTAG or SWD (Serial Wire Debug) interface. These interfaces enable programming, debugging, and real time monitoring of the application. When working with Rust, we can use tools like OpenOCD and GDB to interact with these debug interfaces, allowing us to flash our compiled programs and debug them effectively.

The STM32 ecosystem includes several development board families that make it easier to get started with these microcontrollers. The Discovery and Nucleo boards are particularly popular choices, offering integrated debuggers, user interfaces (LEDs, buttons), and expansion headers for connecting external components. These boards provide an excellent platform for learning embedded Rust development and prototyping applications.

When developing for STM32 in Rust, we have several choices for hardware abstraction. The stm32-hal crates provide low level access to microcontroller peripherals, while maintaining Rust's safety guarantees. These crates are typically generated from SVD (System View Description) files provided by STMicroelectronics, ensuring accurate hardware representations. The embedded-hal trait implementations built on top of these low level crates enable portable code that can work across different STM32 devices.

Power management is a crucial consideration when working with STM32 microcontrollers. Most devices offer various low power modes, from simple sleep states to deep power down modes that can dramatically reduce energy consumption. Rust's type system can help ensure that power management state transitions are handled correctly, preventing many common errors that could lead to unexpected behavior or excessive power consumption.

Clock configuration is another important aspect of STM32 development. These microcontrollers typically feature multiple clock sources and complex clock trees that need to be properly configured for optimal operation. The Rust ecosystem provides abstractions that help manage clock configuration safely, ensuring that peripherals receive appropriate clock signals while maintaining system stability.

Security features are increasingly important in embedded systems, and many STM32 devices include hardware security features such as true random number generators, cryptographic accelerators, and secure boot capabilities. Rust's security focused design philosophy aligns well with these hardware features, making it easier to implement secure applications.

When getting started with STM32 development in Rust, it's important to choose appropriate development tools. In addition to the Rust toolchain, you'll need an ARM GCC toolchain for linking, OpenOCD for debugging, and potentially an IDE or code editor with good Rust support. Many developers use VS Code with rust analyzer, which provides excellent support for embedded Rust development.

The STM32 platform also offers excellent support for real time applications. Many devices include features like deterministic interrupt latency and priority based interrupt handling that are essential for real time systems. Rust's predictable performance characteristics and zero cost abstractions make it particularly well suited for implementing real time applications on STM32 microcontrollers.

Understanding the boot process is crucial when working with STM32 devices. These microcontrollers typically support multiple boot modes, allowing code to be executed from different memory locations. The boot process can be configured using boot pins or option bytes, and proper understanding is essential for implementing reliable firmware updates and secure boot mechanisms.

Looking ahead to the following chapters, we'll explore specific development tools, dig deeper into the hardware abstraction layer, and implement practical projects using STM32 microcontrollers. The combination of STM32's capable hardware platform and Rust's safety features provides an excellent foundation for developing reliable embedded systems.

21. Setting Up STM32 Development Tools

Building on our introduction to the STM32 platform, this chapter focuses on setting up the necessary development tools for STM32 programming with Rust. A proper development environment is crucial for efficient embedded systems development, and we'll walk through the installation and configuration of all required components.

The first essential component is the Rust toolchain itself, specifically configured for ARM Cortex M development. While you may already have Rust installed from previous chapters, we need to ensure we have the appropriate target support for STM32 devices. Using rustup, we'll add the necessary targets with the command "rustup target add thumbv6m-none-eabi thumbv7m-none-eabi thumbv7em-none-eabi thumbv7em-none-eabihf". These targets cover the most common ARM Cortex M cores used in STM32 microcontrollers, from the basic Cortex M0 to the more powerful Cortex M4 and M7 with floating point support.

Next, we need to install the GNU Arm Embedded Toolchain, which provides essential tools for working with ARM-based microcontrollers. This toolchain includes the GCC compiler, linker, and various binary utilities specifically designed for ARM architecture. While Rust handles most of the compilation process, we still need these tools for linking and certain low-level operations. The toolchain can be downloaded from ARM's official website or installed through package managers on most operating systems.

OpenOCD (Open On-Chip Debugger) is another critical tool in our development arsenal. This open-source software provides debugging and in-system programming support for ARM devices, including the entire STM32 family. OpenOCD acts as a bridge between your development computer and the target microcontroller, enabling you to flash firmware, set breakpoints, and inspect program execution. When installing OpenOCD, ensure you get a version that includes STM32 configuration files, which define the specific parameters for different STM32 devices and development boards.

For actual debugging sessions, we'll need GDB (GNU Debugger), specifically the ARM version that comes with the GNU Arm Embedded Toolchain. GDB allows us to perform source-level debugging, stepping through our Rust code line by line, inspecting variables, and analyzing program behavior. The integration between GDB and OpenOCD enables powerful debugging capabilities that are essential for embedded development.

An integrated development environment (IDE) or advanced text editor can significantly improve productivity. Visual Studio Code (VS Code) has become a popular choice for Rust development, offering excellent support through various extensions. The "rust-analyzer" extension provides intelligent code completion, inline hints, and other language-specific features. Additionally, the "Cortex-Debug" extension integrates with OpenOCD and GDB to provide a graphical debugging interface specifically designed for ARM Cortex devices.

Setting up project templates and build configurations is another important aspect of the development environment. The cargo-generate tool can help create new projects from existing templates, saving time when starting new STM32 projects. Many community-maintained templates are available that include appropriate linker scripts, startup code, and basic peripheral initialization for various STM32 devices.

When working with specific STM32 boards, you'll need the corresponding SVD (System View Description) files. These XML files describe the memory map and peripheral registers of the microcontroller, enabling accurate hardware abstractions in Rust. STMicroelectronics provides these files for their devices, and they're often included in the corresponding HAL crates, but having the original files can be useful for reference and custom implementations.

For firmware flashing and basic board interaction, ST-Link tools are essential. The ST-Link is a programming and debugging interface found on many STM32 development boards. While OpenOCD can handle most programming tasks, the official ST-Link tools provide additional functionality and can be useful for recovery operations or when working with protected devices.

Documentation tools are another important consideration. The cargo-doc command can generate documentation for your projects, including the embedded-specific parts. Setting up documentation generation in your build process helps maintain clear API documentation and usage examples, which is particularly important for embedded projects where hardware interactions need to be clearly documented.

Many developers also find it useful to install serial terminal programs for communicating with STM32 devices over UART. Tools like PuTTY, minicom, or the cross-platform serial-monitor provide essential functionality for debugging and monitoring applications that use serial communication.

When working with multiple projects or different STM32 devices, maintaining separate workspace configurations can help organize your development environment. Consider using workspace management tools or creating scripted environments that can switch between different toolchain configurations based on the target device.

For continuous integration and automated testing, additional tools may be necessary. Tools like probe-rs provide a modern, pure Rust alternative to OpenOCD for flashing and debugging. Setting up automated testing using these tools can help catch issues early in the development process.

Version control is crucial for any software development, and embedded projects are no exception. While Git is the standard choice, configuring it properly for embedded projects requires some consideration. Setting up appropriate gitignore files to exclude build artifacts, being careful with binary files, and managing dependencies effectively are all important aspects of version control setup.

The development environment should also include tools for analyzing binary size and performance. The cargo-size and cargo-bloat tools can help track the memory footprint of your applications, which is crucial when working with constrained devices. Additionally, tools for analyzing real-time performance and power consumption may be necessary depending on your project requirements.

Remember to configure your development environment to handle both debug and release builds appropriately. Debug builds should include symbols and debugging information, while release builds should optimize for size and performance. Understanding how to configure these builds and switch between them efficiently is important for productive development.

Finally, consider setting up project-specific tools and scripts to automate common tasks such as flashing firmware, running tests, and generating documentation. These tools can significantly improve development efficiency and help maintain consistent processes across team members.

With all these tools properly installed and configured, you'll have a robust development environment for STM32 programming with Rust. The next chapter will build on this foundation as we explore the STM32 Hardware Abstraction Layer and begin implementing practical applications.

22. STM32 Hardware Abstraction Layer

The STM32 Hardware Abstraction Layer (HAL) serves as a crucial abstraction between your Rust application code and the raw hardware registers of STM32 microcontrollers. Understanding how to effectively use the HAL enables developers to write portable, maintainable code while maintaining the performance characteristics necessary for embedded systems.

At its core, the STM32 HAL provides a safe, Rust-native interface to the microcontroller's peripherals. This abstraction is implemented through several crates, with the primary ones being stm32-hal and the specific device support crates like stm32f4xx-hal. These crates work together to provide a consistent API across different STM32 families while accounting for hardware-specific features and limitations.

The foundation of the HAL system starts with the Peripheral Access Crates (PACs), which are automatically generated from SVD files provided by STMicroelectronics. These crates provide the lowest level of safe access to the hardware registers. Building upon this, the HAL implements higher-level abstractions that handle common configurations and usage patterns while maintaining zero-cost abstractions, ensuring that the resulting code is as efficient as direct register manipulation.

One of the key features of the STM32 HAL is its type-state programming model, which leverages Rust's type system to prevent incorrect peripheral usage at compile time. For example, when working with GPIO pins, the type system ensures that you cannot use a pin configured as an input for output operations. This is achieved through type parameters that track the current state of the pin, making it impossible to perform invalid operations without first reconfiguring the pin appropriately.

Let's examine the clock configuration system as an example of how the HAL provides safe abstractions. STM32 devices have complex clock trees that need careful configuration to achieve desired system frequencies while maintaining proper operation of all peripherals. The HAL provides a builder pattern interface for clock configuration that validates settings at compile time, preventing many common configuration errors that could lead to system malfunction.

The HAL's abstraction of peripheral initialization and configuration is particularly valuable. Take the UART peripheral as an example. Instead of directly manipulating multiple registers with specific bit patterns, the HAL provides a clear, type-safe interface. You can specify parameters like baud rate, word length, and stop bits using natural units and enum values, while the HAL handles the translation to appropriate register values.

Memory-mapped peripherals in STM32 devices are represented in the HAL using Rust's ownership system. When you take ownership of a peripheral through the HAL's APIs, the type system ensures that no other part of your code can simultaneously access that peripheral, preventing race conditions and other concurrency issues. This is particularly important in interrupt-driven applications where multiple parts of the code might attempt to access the same peripheral.

DMA operations, which are crucial for high-performance applications, are also safely abstracted by the HAL. The HAL ensures that memory buffers used for DMA transfers remain valid for the duration of the transfer and provides safe interfaces for configuring and monitoring DMA operations. This prevents common errors like buffer deallocation during active transfers or incorrect memory alignment.

The HAL implements the embedded-hal traits, making it possible to write device-agnostic drivers that work across different microcontroller families. This abstraction allows you to develop reusable components that can work with any microcontroller that implements the same traits. For example, a sensor driver written using the embedded-hal I2C traits can work unchanged across different STM32 families or even entirely different microcontroller architectures.

Error handling in the HAL is designed to be both comprehensive and efficient. Instead of runtime checks that would impact performance, many potential errors are caught at compile time through the type system. For runtime errors that cannot be prevented statically, the HAL uses Rust's Result type to ensure errors are handled explicitly, promoting robust error handling without sacrificing performance.

The HAL provides abstractions for power management features of STM32 devices, including sleep modes and peripheral clock gating. These abstractions make it easier to implement power efficient applications while ensuring that all necessary peripherals remain properly configured and operational. The type system helps prevent common errors like attempting to use a peripheral while its clock is disabled.

Timer peripherals in STM32 devices are abstracted to provide both blocking and non-blocking interfaces. The HAL allows you to configure timers for various purposes, from simple delays to complex PWM generation, while maintaining type safety and preventing invalid configurations. The abstractions handle details like clock prescaling and period calculations while exposing a clean, intuitive API.

When working with external interrupts, the HAL provides safe abstractions that handle the complexity of interrupt configuration and management. This includes proper initialization of the NVIC (Nested Vectored Interrupt Controller) and safe methods for enabling and disabling interrupts. The HAL ensures that interrupt handlers are properly registered and that shared resources are accessed safely in interrupt contexts.

The HAL's abstraction of analog peripherals like ADC and DAC handles the complexity of calibration, sampling time configuration, and conversion sequencing. These abstractions make it easier to implement accurate analog measurements while ensuring proper timing and synchronization requirements are met.

For advanced features like hardware cryptography and random number generation, the HAL provides safe interfaces that handle initialization, key management, and proper usage of these security-sensitive peripherals. This is particularly important for IoT applications where security is a critical concern.

Understanding how to extend the HAL for custom peripherals or specialized functionality is also important. The HAL's design allows for creation of new abstractions that maintain the same level of safety and performance as the built-in features. This extensibility is crucial for complex applications that may require unique hardware interactions not covered by the standard HAL implementation.

The STM32 HAL represents a careful balance between safety, abstraction, and performance. By providing safe, zero-cost abstractions for hardware access, it enables developers to write reliable embedded applications while maintaining the performance characteristics necessary for real-time systems. The next chapter will build upon this foundation as we implement a practical data logging application using these HAL abstractions.

23. STM32 Project: Real-Time Data Logger

Building upon our understanding of the STM32 HAL, let's create a practical real time data logging system that demonstrates how to effectively utilize the HAL abstractions in a real world application. This project will combine multiple peripheral interfaces and demonstrate proper resource management in an embedded context.

Our data logger will capture environmental data from multiple sensors, timestamp the measurements, and store them in external flash memory. This type of application is common in industrial monitoring, scientific research, and IoT deployments where continuous data collection and storage are essential.

Let's begin with the core system architecture. We'll need to interface with several peripherals: I2C for environmental sensors, SPI for external flash memory, RTC for timestamping, and UART for debugging and configuration. The first step is to set up these peripherals using the STM32 HAL.

First, we'll initialize the system clock. For our data logger, we'll configure the system to run at 84MHz, which provides sufficient processing power while maintaining reasonable power consumption. Here's how we configure the clock using the HAL:

```rust
let dp = stm32::Peripherals::take().unwrap();
let rcc = dp.RCC.constrain();
let clocks = rcc.cfgr
.use_hse(8.mhz())
.sysclk(84.mhz())
.pclk1(42.mhz())
.pclk2(84.mhz())
```

```
.freeze();
```

Next, we'll set up our storage system using external flash memory connected via SPI. The W25Q64 flash chip is a common choice for data logging applications, offering 8MB of storage. We'll create a simple ring buffer structure in the flash memory to handle continuous logging:

```rust
let spi = dp.SPI1.spi(
(sck, miso, mosi),
Mode {
polarity: Polarity::IdleLow,
phase: Phase::CaptureOnFirstTransition,
},
1.mhz(),
clocks,
);
struct FlashLogger {
spi: Spi<SPI1>,
current_sector: u32,
sector_offset: u32,
}
```

The environmental sensors will be connected via I2C. We'll use the BME280 for temperature, humidity, and pressure measurements. The HAL makes it straightforward to initialize and communicate with I2C devices:

```rust
let i2c = dp.I2C1.i2c(
(scl, sda),
400.khz(),
clocks,
```

```
);
let mut bme280 = Bme280::new(i2c, 0x76);
bme280.init().unwrap();
```

For accurate timestamping, we'll configure the RTC. The STM32's RTC peripheral provides calendar functionality with battery backup support:

```rust
let rtc = dp.RTC.constrain();
rtc.set_datetime(&DateTime {
year: 2024,
month: 1,
day: 1,
hour: 0,
minute: 0,
second: 0,
});
```

The core logging functionality needs to handle periodic sensor readings, timestamp generation, and data storage. We'll implement this using a timer interrupt to ensure consistent sampling intervals:

```rust
#[interrupt]
fn TIM2() {
static mut LOGGER: Option<DataLogger> = None;
if let Some(logger) = LOGGER {
let timestamp = logger.rtc.now();
let measurements = logger.read_sensors();
logger.store_data(timestamp, measurements);
}
}
```

Data format is crucial for efficient storage and later analysis. We'll define a compact binary format that includes a timestamp and sensor readings:

```rust
#[repr(C, packed)]
struct LogEntry {
timestamp: u32,
temperature: i16,
humidity: u16,
pressure: u32,
}
```

Power management is essential for long term operation. We'll implement several power saving features using the HAL's power management abstractions:

```rust
fn enter_low_power_mode(peripherals: &mut Peripherals) {
peripherals.flash.acr.modify(|_, w| w.latency().bits(0));
peripherals.rcc.cfgr.modify(|_, w| w.ppre1().div1());
peripherals.pwr.cr.modify(|_, w| w.lpds().set_bit());
cortex_m::asm::wfi();
}
```

Error handling is crucial in a data logging system. We'll implement a robust error handling strategy that can recover from common issues:

```rust
enum LoggerError {
SensorError,
StorageError,
TimestampError,
}
```

```
impl DataLogger {
fn handle_error(&mut self, error: LoggerError) {
match error {
LoggerError::SensorError => self.reinitialize_sensors(),
LoggerError::StorageError => self.recover_storage(),
LoggerError::TimestampError => self.sync_rtc(),
}
}
}
```

To enable later data retrieval and analysis, we'll implement a simple command interface over UART:

```rust
fn process_commands(&mut self) {
let mut uart = self.uart.borrow_mut();
match uart.read() {
Ok(b'D') => self.dump_data(),
Ok(b'C') => self.clear_storage(),
Ok(b'S') => self.get_status(),
_ => {},
}
}
```

The complete data logger implementation demonstrates several important embedded development concepts: peripheral initialization and management, interrupt handling, power management, error recovery, and external communications. The HAL abstractions make it possible to implement these features safely while maintaining direct control over the hardware when needed.

Testing and validation are crucial aspects of embedded development. We'll implement a comprehensive test strategy:

```rust
```

```
#[cfg(test)]
mod tests {
use super::*;
#[test]
fn test_sensor_reading() {
let mut logger = DataLogger::new();
assert!(logger.read_sensors().is_ok());
}
#[test]
fn test_storage_operations() {
let mut logger = DataLogger::new();
let data = LogEntry::default();
assert!(logger.store_data(&data).is_ok());
}
}
```

This implementation provides a solid foundation for a real time data logging system. The use of Rust's type system and the STM32 HAL's safety features helps prevent common embedded programming errors while maintaining the performance characteristics necessary for continuous data collection and storage.

In the next chapter, we'll explore another practical application: implementing a motor control system that demonstrates real time control and feedback processing using the STM32 platform.

24. STM32 Project: Motor Control System

Let's create a comprehensive motor control system using the STM32 platform, focusing on precise motion control and real time feedback processing. This project will demonstrate how to use Rust's strong type system and zero cost abstractions to build a reliable and efficient motor controller.

Our motor control system will support both DC and stepper motors, implement PID control, and provide position feedback using encoders. This type of system is commonly found in robotics, CNC machines, and industrial automation applications.

First, let's set up the necessary peripherals. We'll need PWM outputs for motor control, timer inputs for encoder feedback, ADC for current sensing, and communications interfaces for external control:

```rust
let dp = stm32::Peripherals::take().unwrap();
let cp = cortex_m::Peripherals::take().unwrap();
let rcc = dp.RCC.constrain();
let clocks = rcc.cfgr
.use_hse(8.mhz())
.sysclk(84.mhz())
.pclk1(42.mhz())
.pclk2(84.mhz())
.freeze();
let gpioa = dp.GPIOA.split();
let gpiob = dp.GPIOB.split();
```

For PWM generation, we'll configure Timer 2 with multiple channels. This allows us to control multiple motors or implement more complex control schemes like field oriented control:

```rust
struct MotorPWM {
timer: Timer<TIM2>,
channel1: PwmChannel<TIM2, C1>,
channel2: PwmChannel<TIM2, C2>,
frequency: Hertz,
}
impl MotorPWM {
fn new(timer: TIM2, clocks: &Clocks) -> Self {
let frequency = 20.khz();
let mut timer = Timer::new(timer, clocks);
timer.set_frequency(frequency);
let channels = timer.split();
MotorPWM {
timer,
channel1: channels.0,
channel2: channels.1,
frequency,
}
}
}
```

The PID controller is crucial for precise motor control. We'll implement a generic PID controller that can be used for both position and velocity control:

```rust
struct PIDController {
kp: f32,
ki: f32,
```

```
kd: f32,
setpoint: f32,
integral: f32,
previous_error: f32,
output_min: f32,
output_max: f32,
}
impl PIDController {
fn compute(&mut self, current_value: f32, dt: f32) -> f32 {
let error = self.setpoint - current_value;
self.integral += error * dt;
let derivative = (error - self.previous_error) / dt;
let output = self.kp * error +
self.ki * self.integral +
self.kd * derivative;
self.previous_error = error;
output.clamp(self.output_min, self.output_max)
}
}
```

Encoder feedback processing requires careful timing and efficient interrupt handling. We'll use a hardware timer to track encoder pulses:

```rust
struct QuadratureEncoder {
timer: Timer<TIM3>,
position: i32,
velocity: f32,
last_update: u32,
}
impl QuadratureEncoder {
fn update(&mut self) {
```

```rust
let current_count = self.timer.cnt.read().cnt().bits();
let time_diff = self.timer.cnt.read().cnt().bits() - self.last_update;
self.position += current_count as i32;
self.velocity = (current_count as f32) / (time_diff as f32);
self.last_update = current_count;
}
}
```

Current sensing is important for motor protection and torque control. We'll configure the ADC to monitor motor current:

```rust
struct CurrentSensor {
adc: Adc<ADC1>,
pin: Pin<Analog>,
shunt_resistance: f32,
}
impl CurrentSensor {
fn read_current(&mut self) -> f32 {
let raw_value = self.adc.read(&mut self.pin).unwrap();
let voltage = (raw_value as f32 / 4096.0) * 3.3;
voltage / self.shunt_resistance
}
}
```

The main motor control loop needs to run at a fixed frequency to maintain stable control. We'll use a hardware timer to trigger the control updates:

```rust
#[interrupt]
fn TIM4() {
```

```
static mut CONTROLLER: Option<MotorController> = None;
if let Some(controller) = CONTROLLER {
controller.encoder.update();
let current_position = controller.encoder.position;
let output = controller.pid.compute(
current_position as f32,
0.001 // 1ms control period
);
controller.update_motor_output(output);
}
}
```

For stepper motor control, we'll implement a step sequencer that handles microstepping:

```rust
struct StepperController {
current_step: u8,
microsteps: u8,
direction: bool,
pwm: MotorPWM,
}
impl StepperController {
fn step(&mut self) {
let angle = (self.current_step as f32 / self.microsteps as f32) * 2.0 * PI;
let sine = angle.sin();
let cosine = angle.cos();
self.pwm.channel1.set_duty(((sine + 1.0) * 0.5 * self.pwm.max_duty()) as u16);
self.pwm.channel2.set_duty(((cosine + 1.0) * 0.5 * self.pwm.max_duty()) as u16);
```

```
if self.direction {
self.current_step = (self.current_step + 1) % (self.microsteps * 4);
} else {
self.current_step = (self.current_step - 1) % (self.microsteps * 4);
}
}
}
```

Safety features are crucial in motor control applications. We'll implement various protection mechanisms:

```rust
struct MotorProtection {
max_current: f32,
max_temperature: f32,
current_sensor: CurrentSensor,
temperature_sensor: Option<TemperatureSensor>,
}
impl MotorProtection {
fn check_safety(&mut self) -> Result<(), MotorError> {
let current = self.current_sensor.read_current();
if current > self.max_current {
return Err(MotorError::OverCurrent);
}
if let Some(temp_sensor) = &mut self.temperature_sensor {
let temperature = temp_sensor.read_temperature();
if temperature > self.max_temperature {
return Err(MotorError::OverTemperature);
}
}
Ok(())
}
```

```
}
```

The complete motor control system demonstrates advanced embedded programming concepts including real time control, interrupt handling, analog signal processing, and safety management. The use of Rust's type system helps prevent many common errors while maintaining the performance necessary for motor control applications.

This implementation provides a solid foundation for building more complex motion control systems. In the next chapter, we'll explore programming the Raspberry Pi with Rust, shifting our focus to Linux based embedded development.

25. Raspberry Pi Programming with Rust

Chapter 25 continues the journey into embedded Rust development by exploring programming on the Raspberry Pi platform. Unlike our previous microcontroller projects, the Raspberry Pi provides a full Linux environment, offering different challenges and opportunities for embedded development.

The Raspberry Pi represents a significant shift in our embedded programming approach. While microcontrollers like the Arduino and STM32 require bare metal programming, the Raspberry Pi runs a complete operating system, allowing us to leverage higher level abstractions while still maintaining close hardware control when needed.

Let's begin by examining how to set up Rust development environment specifically for Raspberry Pi. While you can develop directly on the Pi, a cross compilation workflow often proves more efficient. First, we'll need to add the appropriate target to our Rust toolchain:

```rust
rustup target add armv7 unknown linux gnueabihf
```

For GPIO access on the Raspberry Pi, we'll use the rppal crate, which provides safe abstractions over the hardware interfaces. This crate allows us to work with GPIO, I2C, SPI, and UART without dealing directly with memory mapped registers. Here's a basic example of GPIO control:

```rust
use rppal::gpio::Gpio;
let gpio = Gpio::new().unwrap();
let mut pin = gpio.get(18).unwrap().into_output();
pin.set_high();
```

One of the key advantages of developing for Raspberry Pi is the ability to use standard Linux networking stacks and higher level protocols. We can create network enabled applications using standard Rust libraries like tokio for asynchronous IO:

```rust
use tokio::net::TcpListener;
#[tokio::main]
async fn main() {
let listener = TcpListener::bind("0.0.0.0:8080").await.unwrap();
loop {
let (socket, _) = listener.accept().await.unwrap();
tokio::spawn(async move {
handle_connection(socket).await;
});
}
}
```

Hardware access on the Raspberry Pi often involves working with various buses and protocols. The Linux sysfs interface provides access to many hardware features, but we can also use direct memory mapping when needed. Here's an example of working with the I2C bus:

```rust
use rppal::i2c::I2c;
struct I2CDevice {
i2c: I2c,
address: u8,
}
impl I2CDevice {
fn new(bus: u8, address: u8) -> Result<Self, rppal::i2c::Error> {
let i2c = I2c::new()?;
i2c.set_slave_address(address as u16)?;
```

```
Ok(I2CDevice {
i2c,
address,
})
}
fn read_register(&mut self, register: u8) -> Result<u8, rppal::i2c::Error> {
let mut buffer = [0u8; 1];
self.i2c.write_read(&[register], &mut buffer)?;
Ok(buffer[0])
}
}
```

Real time capabilities on the Raspberry Pi require careful consideration. While it's not a real time system by default, we can achieve reasonable real time performance for many applications. Using thread priorities and proper scheduling can help:

```rust
use nix::sched::{sched_setscheduler, SchedParams, sched_get_priority_max};
use nix::sys::time::{TimeSpec, TimeValLike};
fn set_realtime_priority() -> Result<(), nix::Error> {
let priority = sched_get_priority_max(nix::sched::SCHED_FIFO)?;
sched_setscheduler(
0,
nix::sched::SCHED_FIFO,
&SchedParams::new(priority)
)
}
```

The Raspberry Pi's multimedia capabilities also open up interesting possibilities for embedded applications. We can access the camera module using the raspicam interface:

```rust
use rascam::{SimpleCamera, Config};
struct CameraController {
camera: SimpleCamera,
config: Config,
}
impl CameraController {
fn new() -> Result<Self, rascam::Error> {
let mut config = Config::new()?;
config.set_resolution(1920, 1080);
config.set_framerate(30);
let camera = SimpleCamera::new(config.clone())?;
Ok(CameraController {
camera,
config,
})
}
fn capture_frame(&mut self) -> Result<Vec<u8>,
rascam::Error> {
self.camera.take_picture()
}
}
```

Memory management on the Raspberry Pi differs significantly from microcontroller development. While we still need to be mindful of resource usage, we have access to the Linux memory management system:

```rust
use std::alloc::{GlobalAlloc, Layout, System};
```

```
struct ResourceMonitor;
unsafe impl GlobalAlloc for ResourceMonitor {
unsafe fn alloc(&self, layout: Layout) -> *mut u8 {
let ptr = System.alloc(layout);
// Log allocation size and address
ptr
}
unsafe fn dealloc(&self, ptr: *mut u8, layout: Layout) {
System.dealloc(ptr, layout);
// Log deallocation
}
}
```

Process management and interprocess communication are important considerations for Raspberry Pi applications. We can use standard Unix primitives or higher level abstractions:

```rust
use std::process::Command;
use ipc_channel::ipc;
fn spawn_worker_process() -> Result<(), Box<dyn std::error::Error>> {
let (tx, rx) = ipc::channel()?;
let child = Command::new("/usr/bin/worker")
.arg(tx.as_raw_fd().to_string())
.spawn()?;
for message in rx.iter() {
handle_worker_message(message);
}
Ok(())
}
```

The Raspberry Pi's Linux environment also provides excellent debugging capabilities. We can use standard debugging tools and logging frameworks:

```rust
use tracing::{info, error, Level};
use tracing_subscriber::FmtSubscriber;
fn setup_logging() {
let subscriber = FmtSubscriber::builder()
.with_max_level(Level::TRACE)
.with_file(true)
.with_line_number(true)
.with_thread_ids(true)
.init();
}
```

Finally, we should consider security implications when developing for the Raspberry Pi. Unlike microcontrollers, the Pi is often network connected and runs a full operating system:

```rust
use users::{get_current_uid, get_user_by_uid};
use caps::{Capability, CapSet};
fn drop_privileges() -> Result<(), Box<dyn std::error::Error>>
{
let uid = get_current_uid();
if uid == 0 {
// Drop capabilities we don't need
caps::clear(None, CapSet::Effective)?;
// Switch to non root user
let user = get_user_by_uid(1000)
.ok_or("Cannot find non root user")?;
nix::unistd::setuid(user.uid())?;
}
```

```
    Ok(())
}
```

The Raspberry Pi provides a powerful platform for embedded development with Rust, combining the safety and expressiveness of Rust with the capabilities of a Linux system. This allows us to build sophisticated embedded applications while maintaining good performance and reliability. In the next chapter, we'll explore Linux based embedded development in more detail, focusing on system integration and advanced Linux features.

26. Linux-Based Embedded Development

Moving beyond bare metal and RTOS-based systems, this chapter explores the world of embedded Linux development using Rust. While previous chapters focused on microcontroller-based systems, embedded Linux opens up new possibilities for more complex applications while still maintaining the safety and performance benefits that Rust provides.

• • • •

EMBEDDED LINUX DEVELOPMENT differs significantly from traditional embedded systems programming. Instead of directly accessing hardware registers and managing every aspect of the system, we work with a full operating system that provides hardware abstraction, process management, and a rich set of system services. This higher-level environment allows us to create more sophisticated applications while leveraging Linux's robust driver support and networking capabilities.

• • • •

THE LINUX ECOSYSTEM brings both advantages and challenges to embedded Rust development. We benefit from Linux's extensive hardware support, standardized interfaces, and proven reliability, but must also consider system resource management, process isolation, and interprocess communication. Rust's ownership model and thread safety guarantees become particularly valuable when dealing with concurrent operations and shared resources in a Linux environment.

• • • •

CROSS-COMPILATION FORMS a crucial aspect of embedded Linux development. We'll explore setting up a cross-compilation environment for various target architectures, such as ARM or RISC-V. This includes configuring toolchains, managing dependencies, and establishing efficient development workflows. Rust's cargo build system simplifies many aspects of cross-compilation, but understanding the underlying mechanisms remains important for effective development.

• • • •

SYSTEM CALLS AND KERNEL interfaces represent the primary means of interacting with hardware in embedded Linux. We'll examine how to use Rust's foreign function interface (FFI) to interact with Linux system calls safely and efficiently. This includes handling file operations, managing devices through sysfs and device trees, and interfacing with hardware through standard Linux interfaces like I2C, SPI, and GPIO subsystems.

• • • •

RESOURCE MANAGEMENT takes on new dimensions in embedded Linux systems. Unlike bare metal systems where we have complete control over memory allocation, we must now consider process memory limits, shared memory regions, and system resource constraints. Rust's ownership model helps prevent memory leaks and race conditions, while its zero-cost abstractions ensure efficient resource usage.

• • • •

DEVICE DRIVERS AND kernel modules represent a specialized area of embedded Linux development. While most applications run in userspace, understanding how to interact with custom drivers and potentially developing kernel modules in Rust provides valuable insights into the Linux system architecture. We'll explore best practices for userspace device interaction and discuss the emerging possibilities for Rust in kernel development.

• • • •

NETWORKING CAPABILITIES significantly expand the potential of embedded Linux systems. We'll implement network services using Rust's async/await syntax and popular networking crates. This includes handling TCP/IP communications, implementing web services, and managing secure network connections. Rust's strong type system helps prevent common networking vulnerabilities while maintaining high performance.

• • • •

SECURITY CONSIDERATIONS become paramount when developing for networked Linux systems. We'll examine implementing secure communication protocols, managing user permissions, and protecting sensitive data. Rust's security features combine with Linux's security mechanisms to create robust, attack-resistant systems. This includes implementing proper privilege separation, secure storage, and authenticated communication channels.

• • • •

PROCESS MANAGEMENT and interprocess communication (IPC) play crucial roles in embedded Linux applications. We'll explore creating and managing child processes, implementing various IPC mechanisms, and handling signals. Rust's threading model and synchronization primitives integrate well with Linux's process management capabilities, allowing us to create complex yet maintainable multi-process applications.

• • • •

REAL-TIME CAPABILITIES, while not as precise as bare metal systems, remain important in many embedded Linux applications. We'll examine techniques for achieving better real-time performance, including process scheduling, interrupt handling, and kernel configuration. This includes working with the PREEMPT_RT patch when strict timing requirements must be met.

• • • •

SYSTEM MONITORING AND debugging take different forms in embedded Linux compared to bare metal systems. We'll explore using Linux's rich set of debugging and profiling tools with Rust applications. This includes integrating with systemd for service management, implementing proper logging, and using performance analysis tools to optimize our applications.

• • • •

STORAGE MANAGEMENT presents unique challenges in embedded Linux systems. We'll examine working with various filesystem types, implementing proper storage handling, and managing system updates. Rust's strong type system helps prevent common filesystem-related errors while providing efficient access to storage resources.

• • • •

POWER MANAGEMENT BECOMES more complex with embedded Linux, involving both system-level and application-level considerations. We'll explore implementing power-aware applications that can respond to system power states and manage their own power consumption efficiently. This includes handling system suspend/resume cycles and implementing power-saving strategies.

• • • •

BY THE END OF THIS chapter, readers will understand how to effectively develop Rust applications for embedded Linux systems. We've seen how Rust's safety features and performance characteristics complement Linux's capabilities, creating a powerful platform for sophisticated embedded applications. The combination of Rust's modern development features with Linux's mature ecosystem provides an excellent foundation for building complex, reliable embedded systems.

• • • •

THIS EXPLORATION OF Linux-based embedded development demonstrates that Rust is well-suited for creating robust applications in more complex embedded environments. Whether developing system services, networked applications, or user interfaces, Rust's safety guarantees and performance characteristics make it an excellent choice for embedded Linux development.

27. Raspberry Pi Project: IoT Gateway

Building an IoT gateway with a Raspberry Pi serves as an excellent introduction to real world IoT applications, combining the reliability of Rust with the versatility of this popular single board computer. In this chapter, we'll develop a comprehensive IoT gateway that can collect data from various sensors, process it, and forward it to cloud services while maintaining robust security and efficient performance.

Our IoT gateway will serve as a bridge between local sensor networks and the broader internet, handling protocol translation, data aggregation, and secure communication. We'll start by setting up the basic infrastructure using Rust's powerful async runtime Tokio, which is particularly well suited for handling multiple concurrent connections and data streams.

First, let's establish the core functionality of our gateway. We'll need to implement multiple communication interfaces to handle both upstream and downstream connections. On the local side, we'll create listeners for various protocols that IoT devices commonly use, including MQTT, CoAP, and simple HTTP endpoints. The following code structure demonstrates the basic setup:

```rust
use tokio;
use rumqttc;
use hyper;
struct IoTGateway {
mqtt_broker: MqttBroker,
http_server: HttpServer,
device_registry: DeviceRegistry,
data_buffer: DataBuffer,
}
```

The device registry is crucial for maintaining a list of authorized devices and their capabilities. We'll implement it with Rust's strong type system to ensure data consistency and proper access control. The data buffer provides temporary storage for situations where internet connectivity might be interrupted, preventing data loss during network outages.

Security is paramount in IoT applications, so we'll implement TLS for all external communications. Rust's strong security guarantees help prevent common vulnerabilities, and we'll use the rustls crate for efficient and secure TLS implementations. We'll also implement device authentication using X.509 certificates and maintain a secure key storage system.

One of the most important aspects of our gateway is efficient data handling. We'll implement a smart buffering system that can aggregate data from multiple sources and optimize transmission to reduce bandwidth usage and power consumption. This is particularly important when dealing with battery powered sensor nodes that communicate with the gateway.

The data processing pipeline will include filtering, transformation, and validation stages. We'll use Rust's powerful trait system to create flexible and reusable components that can be easily configured for different use cases. For example, we might implement a trait for data transformers:

```rust
trait DataTransformer {
fn transform(&self, data: &SensorData) -> Result<TransformedData, TransformError>;
fn validate(&self, data: &TransformedData) -> bool;
}
```

Error handling is crucial in gateway applications, as we need to gracefully handle various failure scenarios without losing data or compromising security. We'll implement comprehensive error handling and logging systems that can help diagnose issues and maintain system stability.

The gateway will also include a local web interface for configuration and monitoring. We'll use the Yew framework to create a reactive web interface that can display real time statistics and allow administrators to configure gateway parameters. This interface will be secured with proper authentication and authorization mechanisms.

For cloud connectivity, we'll implement support for major cloud providers including AWS IoT Core, Azure IoT Hub, and Google Cloud IoT Core. We'll create abstractions that make it easy to switch between different cloud providers or use multiple providers simultaneously:

```rust
trait CloudProvider {
async fn connect(&mut self) -> Result<(), CloudError>;
async fn send_data(&self, data: &ProcessedData) -> Result<(), CloudError>;
async fn receive_commands(&self) -> Result<Command, CloudError>;
}
```

The gateway will support device provisioning and management, including firmware updates for connected devices. We'll implement a secure update mechanism that can verify firmware signatures and ensure atomic updates to prevent devices from entering an inconsistent state.

Performance monitoring is essential for maintaining a healthy IoT system. We'll implement metrics collection using the prometheus crate and create dashboards that can help identify bottlenecks and potential issues before they become critical problems.

To handle scale, we'll implement proper resource management techniques. This includes connection pooling, rate limiting, and load shedding when necessary. We'll use Rust's ownership system to ensure resources are properly managed and released when no longer needed.

The final component of our gateway is the configuration system. We'll implement a flexible configuration mechanism that can be updated at runtime, allowing for dynamic adjustment of gateway behavior without requiring restarts. This includes adjusting buffer sizes, connection limits, and protocol specific parameters.

Testing is crucial for gateway reliability. We'll create a comprehensive test suite that includes unit tests, integration tests, and load tests. We'll also implement chaos testing scenarios to ensure the gateway can handle various failure modes gracefully.

Our implementation will include proper logging and monitoring capabilities, using the tracing crate for structured logging that can help with debugging and performance analysis. We'll also implement health checks and watchdog functionality to ensure the gateway can recover from failures automatically.

The completed IoT gateway will be capable of handling thousands of connected devices while maintaining security and reliability. It can serve as a foundation for various IoT applications, from smart home systems to industrial monitoring solutions. The use of Rust ensures that common security vulnerabilities are prevented at compile time, while still providing the performance needed for handling high throughput data streams.

This chapter provides a practical example of how Rust's safety features and performance characteristics make it an excellent choice for IoT infrastructure components. The gateway implementation demonstrates real world usage of many Rust features we've covered in previous chapters, including async programming, trait based abstractions, and strong type safety.

In the next chapter, we'll explore how to extend this gateway with camera interface capabilities, allowing for video streaming and image processing applications. This will demonstrate how our gateway architecture can be extended to handle more complex data types and processing requirements.

28. Raspberry Pi Project: Camera Interface

Chapter 28 focuses on implementing a camera interface using Rust on the Raspberry Pi, building upon our knowledge of embedded systems and extending our IoT capabilities to include image processing and video streaming. This practical implementation demonstrates how to leverage Rust's safety features while handling real time video data.

The Raspberry Pi's camera module provides an excellent platform for learning about video capture and processing in embedded systems. We'll begin by setting up the necessary hardware interfaces using the libcamera framework, which has replaced the legacy raspistill and raspivid tools in modern Raspberry Pi systems.

First, let's establish the basic structure for our camera interface. We'll use the rascam crate, which provides safe Rust bindings to the Raspberry Pi camera system:

```rust
use rascam::{SimpleCamera, Config};
use image::{ImageBuffer, Rgb};
struct CameraSystem {
camera: SimpleCamera,
frame_buffer: Vec<u8>,
processing_pipeline: ImageProcessor,
stream_manager: StreamManager,
}
```

The camera initialization process requires careful handling of hardware resources. We'll implement proper resource management using Rust's RAII principles to ensure camera resources are correctly released when no longer needed. This is particularly important in long running applications where resource leaks could cause system instability.

Image capture in our system will support multiple modes, including still image capture and video streaming. For still images, we'll implement a capture system that can handle different resolutions and formats:

```rust
impl CameraSystem {
async fn capture_still(&mut self, resolution: Resolution) -> Result<ImageBuffer<Rgb<u8>>> {
let raw_data = self.camera.capture_frame()?;
let processed_image = self.processing_pipeline.process_raw_data(raw_data)?;
Ok(processed_image)
}
}
```

Video streaming presents more complex challenges, particularly in terms of memory management and real time processing requirements. We'll implement a circular buffer system to manage frame data efficiently, preventing memory exhaustion during long running streaming sessions:

```rust
struct StreamBuffer {
frames: Vec<Frame>,
write_index: usize,
read_index: usize,
capacity: usize,
}
```

Real time image processing is crucial for many applications. We'll implement a processing pipeline that can handle operations like color correction, exposure adjustment, and basic computer vision tasks. The pipeline will be configurable and extensible through a trait based system:

```rust
trait ImageProcessor {
fn process_frame(&self, frame: &Frame) -> Result<ProcessedFrame>;
fn add_filter(&mut self, filter: Box<dyn ImageFilter>);
}
```

Performance optimization is critical when dealing with video data. We'll leverage Rust's zero cost abstractions and SIMD operations where available to maximize processing efficiency. The implementation will include careful memory management to minimize allocations during video streaming:

```rust
impl StreamManager {
fn process_frame_batch(&mut self, frames: &[Frame]) -> Result<Vec<ProcessedFrame>> {
frames.par_iter()
.map(|frame| self.process_single_frame(frame))
.collect()
}
}
```

Network streaming capabilities are essential for many camera applications. We'll implement support for common streaming protocols like RTSP and WebRTC, using Rust's async runtime to handle network operations efficiently:

```rust
struct VideoStream {
codec: VideoCodec,
```

```
transport: StreamTransport,
quality_manager: QualityManager,
}
```

The quality manager will dynamically adjust streaming parameters based on network conditions and client capabilities. This includes implementing adaptive bitrate streaming and handling network congestion gracefully.

Error handling in camera applications requires special attention due to the real time nature of video processing. We'll implement comprehensive error recovery mechanisms:

```rust
enum CameraError {
HardwareError(String),
BufferOverflow,
ProcessingError(String),
StreamingError(NetworkError),
}
```

Security considerations are paramount, especially when streaming video data. We'll implement encryption for all network streams and proper authentication mechanisms for accessing the camera feed:

```rust
struct SecurityManager {
authentication: AuthenticationHandler,
encryption: EncryptionHandler,
access_control: AccessController,
}
```

Motion detection and basic computer vision capabilities can be valuable in many applications. We'll implement these features using the image crate and optional OpenCV bindings through opencv-rust:

```rust
struct MotionDetector {
threshold: f32,
history: VecDeque<Frame>,
detection_algorithm: Box<dyn MotionDetectionAlgorithm>,
}
```

Configuration management will allow users to adjust camera parameters dynamically. We'll implement a configuration system that can be updated through a REST API or configuration file:

```rust
struct CameraConfig {
resolution: Resolution,
framerate: u32,
exposure: ExposureSettings,
white_balance: WhiteBalance,
}
```

Testing camera applications presents unique challenges. We'll create a comprehensive test suite that includes unit tests for image processing algorithms and integration tests using recorded video sequences:

```rust
#[cfg(test)]
mod tests {
use super::*;
#[test]
fn test_image_processing_pipeline() {
// Test implementation
}
```

```
}
```

The completed camera interface system provides a robust foundation for building video enabled IoT applications. It demonstrates how Rust's safety features can be applied to complex real time systems while maintaining high performance and reliability.

This implementation can be extended for various applications including security systems, machine vision, and automated inspection systems. The modular design allows for easy addition of new features while maintaining the safety guarantees that Rust provides.

In the next chapter, we'll explore networking fundamentals for IoT devices, building upon our camera interface to implement network enabled features and remote control capabilities.

29. Networking Fundamentals for IoT

Chapter 29 delves into the fundamental networking concepts essential for IoT devices, providing a comprehensive understanding of how to implement network connectivity in embedded Rust applications.

Networking is a cornerstone of IoT devices, enabling them to communicate, share data, and respond to remote commands. In embedded systems, networking presents unique challenges due to resource constraints and reliability requirements. Rust's strong type system and memory safety guarantees make it particularly well suited for implementing robust networking solutions.

Let's begin by examining the basic networking stack components that are commonly used in IoT applications. The standard networking model follows the TCP/IP protocol suite, but embedded systems often require careful consideration of resource usage and power consumption. We'll use the embedded_nal (Network Abstraction Layer) crate, which provides a common interface for different network implementations:

```rust
use embedded_nal::{TcpClientStack, UdpClientStack};
struct NetworkManager<T: TcpClientStack + UdpClientStack> {
stack: T,
connection_pool: ConnectionPool,
retry_policy: RetryPolicy,
}
```

Connection management is crucial in embedded systems where resources are limited. We'll implement a connection pool that efficiently manages network connections and handles connection lifecycle:

```rust
struct ConnectionPool {
active_connections: Vec<Connection>,
max_connections: usize,
timeout_settings: TimeoutConfig,
}
```

Error handling in networking requires special attention. Network operations can fail for numerous reasons, and our implementation must handle these failures gracefully while maintaining system stability:

```rust
enum NetworkError {
ConnectionFailed(ConnectError),
Timeout(Duration),
InvalidAddress,
StackError(StackError),
}
```

Many IoT applications require support for multiple network protocols. We'll implement handlers for common protocols including HTTP, MQTT, and CoAP:

```rust
trait ProtocolHandler {
fn handle_message(&mut self, message: &[u8]) -> Result<Response>;
fn format_request(&self, request: &Request) -> Result<Vec<u8>>;
}
```

Quality of Service (QoS) is essential for reliable IoT communication. We'll implement QoS mechanisms including message acknowledgment, retransmission, and delivery guarantees:

```rust
struct QosManager {
reliability_level: QosLevel,
retry_count: u32,
acknowledgment_timeout: Duration,
}
```

Power efficiency is critical in battery operated devices. Our networking implementation includes power aware features that can adjust behavior based on power state:

```rust
struct PowerAwareNetwork {
power_state: PowerState,
transmission_power: TransmissionPower,
duty_cycle: f32,
}
```

Network discovery and service advertisement are important for IoT devices that need to be easily discoverable on the network. We'll implement mDNS and DNS SD support:

```rust
struct DiscoveryService {
service_type: ServiceType,
instance_name: String,
port: u16,
txt_records: HashMap<String, String>,
}
```

Security is paramount in networked devices. We'll implement basic security features including TLS support and certificate management:

```rust
struct SecurityLayer {
tls_config: TlsConfig,
certificate_store: CertStore,
key_manager: KeyManager,
}
```

Network diagnostics and monitoring capabilities help in troubleshooting and maintaining deployed devices. We'll implement logging and monitoring features:

```rust
struct NetworkMonitor {
metrics: NetworkMetrics,
event_logger: EventLogger,
alert_system: AlertManager,
}
```

Many IoT applications require reliable message delivery even in unreliable network conditions. We'll implement a store and forward mechanism:

```rust
struct MessageQueue {
pending_messages: VecDeque<Message>,
delivery_guarantees: DeliveryGuarantees,
storage: PersistentStorage,
}
```

Network configuration management allows devices to adapt to different network environments. We'll implement a configuration system that supports both static and dynamic configuration:

```rust
struct NetworkConfig {
ip_settings: IpConfig,
dns_servers: Vec<IpAddr>,
network_mode: NetworkMode,
}
```

Testing networking code requires special consideration. We'll create a test framework that can simulate various network conditions and failure scenarios:

```rust
#[cfg(test)]
mod tests {
use super::*;
struct MockNetwork {
latency: Duration,
packet_loss: f32,
bandwidth: u32,
}
}
```

The networking implementation provides a robust foundation for IoT connectivity while maintaining Rust's safety guarantees. It handles common networking challenges including connection management, error handling, and security while remaining efficient and reliable.

This networking foundation can be extended to support various IoT protocols and use cases. The modular design allows for easy adaptation to different network environments and requirements while maintaining consistent behavior and reliability.

In the next chapter, we'll build upon these networking fundamentals to implement a complete TCP/IP stack, enabling even more sophisticated network capabilities for our IoT devices.

30. Implementing TCP/IP Stack

Building upon our networking fundamentals, implementing a TCP/IP stack in embedded Rust requires careful consideration of memory constraints, performance requirements, and reliability. A custom TCP/IP stack implementation gives us complete control over network behavior and enables optimization for specific use cases.

Let's start with the fundamental components of our TCP/IP stack implementation. At its core, we need to handle IP packet processing, TCP connection management, and provide an interface for higher level protocols. We'll implement this using a layered approach that mirrors the traditional network stack architecture.

The IP layer handles packet routing and addressing. Our implementation supports both IPv4 and IPv6, allowing devices to operate in modern network environments:

```rust
struct IpStack {
routing_table: RoutingTable,
interface_manager: NetworkInterfaces,
packet_buffer: PacketBuffer,
}
impl IpStack {
fn process_packet(&mut self, packet: &[u8]) -> Result<(), NetworkError> {
let header = IpHeader::parse(packet)?;
if header.is_fragment() {
self.handle_fragmentation(header, packet)?;
}
self.forward_packet(header, packet)
}
}
```

```

TCP connection management is critical for reliable communication. We implement a connection state machine that handles the complete TCP lifecycle including connection establishment, data transfer, and graceful termination:

```rust
struct TcpConnection {
state: TcpState,
send_window: Window,
receive_window: Window,
sequence_number: u32,
acknowledgment_number: u32,
}
impl TcpConnection {
fn handle_segment(&mut self, segment: TcpSegment) -> Result<(), TcpError> {
match self.state {
TcpState::Listen => self.handle_listen_state(segment),
TcpState::SynReceived => self.handle_syn_received(segment),
TcpState::Established => self.handle_established(segment),
// Handle other states
}
}
}
```

Flow control and congestion control mechanisms prevent network congestion and ensure efficient data transfer. Our implementation uses a sliding window protocol with adaptive window sizing:

```rust
struct FlowController {
congestion_window: u32,

```rust
slow_start_threshold: u32,
round_trip_time: Duration,
rtt_variance: Duration,
}
impl FlowController {
fn update_window(&mut self, ack: Acknowledgment) {
if self.congestion_window < self.slow_start_threshold {
self.congestion_window *= 2; // Slow start
} else {
self.congestion_window += 1; // Congestion avoidance
}
}
}
```

Memory management is crucial in embedded systems. We implement a zero copy buffer management system that minimizes memory usage and copying operations:

```rust
struct PacketBuffer {
pools: Vec<MemoryPool>,
allocation_strategy: AllocationStrategy,
}
impl PacketBuffer {
fn allocate(&mut self, size: usize) -> Option<Buffer> {
let pool = self.select_pool(size)?;
pool.allocate()
}
fn release(&mut self, buffer: Buffer) {
let pool = self.get_pool_for_buffer(&buffer);
pool.release(buffer);
}
}
```

Checksum calculation and verification ensure data integrity. We implement hardware accelerated checksums where available, falling back to software implementation when necessary:

```rust
trait ChecksumCalculator {
fn calculate(&self, data: &[u8]) -> u16;
fn verify(&self, data: &[u8], expected: u16) -> bool;
}
struct HardwareChecksum {
peripheral: ChecksumPeripheral,
}
struct SoftwareChecksum;
```

Timer management is essential for various TCP operations including retransmission and keepalive mechanisms. We implement an efficient timer system that minimizes overhead:

```rust
struct TimerWheel {
slots: Vec<LinkedList<Timer>>,
current_tick: u64,
resolution: Duration,
}
impl TimerWheel {
fn schedule(&mut self, timeout: Duration, callback: Box<dyn FnOnce()>) {
let ticks = timeout.as_millis() / self.resolution.as_millis();
let slot = ((self.current_tick + ticks) % self.slots.len() as u64) as usize;
self.slots[slot].push_back(Timer::new(callback));
}
}
```

Socket management provides the interface between applications and the network stack. We implement a flexible socket API that supports both blocking and non blocking operations:

```rust
struct Socket {
socket_type: SocketType,
local_address: SocketAddr,
remote_address: Option<SocketAddr>,
state: SocketState,
receive_buffer: RingBuffer,
send_buffer: RingBuffer,
}
impl Socket {
fn connect(&mut self, addrcss: SocketAddr) -> Result<(), SocketError> {
match self.socket_type {
SocketType::Stream => self.tcp_connect(address),
SocketType::Dgram => self.udp_connect(address),
}
}
}
```

Error recovery mechanisms handle various network failure scenarios. We implement automatic retransmission and connection recovery features:

```rust
struct RetransmissionQueue {
unacked_segments: VecDeque&lt;Segment&gt;,
retransmission_timeout: Duration,
backoff_multiplier: f32,
}
```

```
impl RetransmissionQueue {
fn handle_timeout(&mut self) {
self.retransmission_timeout *= self.backoff_multiplier;
self.retransmit_segments();
}
}
```

The complete TCP/IP stack implementation provides a robust foundation for network communication while maintaining strict resource usage controls. It handles all aspects of network communication including connection management, flow control, error recovery, and data integrity verification.

This implementation can be customized for specific embedded applications by adjusting buffer sizes, timing parameters, and enabling or disabling optional features. The modular design allows for easy integration with different hardware platforms and network interfaces.

In the next chapter, we'll explore Bluetooth Low Energy programming, adding another important wireless communication capability to our embedded Rust applications.

31. Bluetooth Low Energy Programming

The integration of Bluetooth Low Energy (BLE) capabilities into embedded systems has become increasingly crucial in modern IoT applications. In this chapter, we explore implementing BLE communication using Rust, focusing on creating energy-efficient, reliable wireless connections while maintaining the safety guarantees that Rust provides.

• • • •

BLE DIFFERS SIGNIFICANTLY from classic Bluetooth, emphasizing low power consumption and simplified connection patterns. We'll examine the core BLE concepts - services, characteristics, advertisements, and the GATT (Generic Attribute Profile) hierarchy. Understanding these fundamentals is crucial for implementing effective BLE communication in Rust, where we can leverage the type system to enforce correct usage of these protocols.

• • • •

OUR RUST IMPLEMENTATION begins with the BLE stack configuration. We'll use the btleplug crate, which provides a cross-platform Bluetooth API that abstracts away many platform-specific details while maintaining high performance. The crate's design aligns well with Rust's ownership model, ensuring that connection states and data transfers are handled safely and efficiently.

• • • •

ADVERTISEMENT HANDLING forms a critical aspect of BLE communication. We'll implement both advertising and scanning functionality, showing how to create discoverable devices and detect nearby BLE peripherals. Rust's strong typing helps prevent common errors in advertisement data formatting while ensuring efficient packet construction. We'll explore setting up advertisement parameters, managing scan responses, and implementing proper power management during discovery phases.

• • • •

CONNECTION MANAGEMENT in BLE requires careful attention to state handling and timing. We'll implement robust connection establishment procedures, including handling connection parameters, managing timeouts, and dealing with disconnection events. Rust's Result type proves particularly valuable here, helping us handle the various error conditions that can occur during connection establishment and maintenance.

• • • •

GATT SERVICE IMPLEMENTATION represents the core of most BLE applications. We'll create custom services and characteristics, implementing both read and write capabilities with proper permissions. Our implementation will showcase how Rust's trait system can create clean abstractions for different types of characteristics while maintaining type safety. We'll also handle notifications and indications, crucial for real-time data updates.

• • • •

SECURITY IN BLE COMMUNICATIONS cannot be overlooked. We'll implement proper pairing mechanisms, including handling encryption keys and managing secure connections. Rust's security features help prevent common vulnerabilities while implementing BLE security protocols. We'll cover both legacy pairing and LE Secure Connections, showing how to implement each securely.

• • • •

POWER MANAGEMENT BECOMES particularly crucial in BLE applications. We'll explore implementing efficient connection parameters, managing advertisement intervals, and optimizing data transmission patterns to minimize power consumption. Rust's zero-cost abstractions ensure that our power management code remains efficient while being easy to understand and maintain.

• • • •

ERROR HANDLING IN BLE communications requires special attention due to the wireless nature of the protocol. We'll implement comprehensive error recovery mechanisms, including handling connection drops, transmission failures, and protocol errors. Rust's error handling patterns help create robust recovery procedures while maintaining system stability.

• • • •

DATA THROUGHPUT OPTIMIZATION presents unique challenges in BLE applications. We'll examine techniques for maximizing transfer rates while maintaining power efficiency, including proper MTU negotiation, connection parameter optimization, and data chunking strategies. We'll implement these optimizations while maintaining type safety and preventing common programming errors.

• • • •

TESTING BLE APPLICATIONS requires specialized approaches. We'll develop testing strategies that include unit testing for protocol handling, integration testing with real devices, and simulation-based testing for complex scenarios. This includes creating mock BLE devices for testing and implementing proper test coverage for wireless communication paths.

• • • •

INTEROPERABILITY REPRESENTS a crucial aspect of BLE development. We'll explore implementing standard BLE profiles and services to ensure compatibility with other devices. This includes handling different versions of the BLE specification and implementing fallback mechanisms for devices with varying capabilities. Rust's type system helps manage these compatibility layers effectively.

• • • •

REAL-TIME CONSTRAINTS often apply in BLE applications, particularly when dealing with sensor data or control systems. We'll implement timing-sensitive BLE operations while maintaining system responsiveness. This includes handling connection events, managing data buffering, and ensuring consistent transmission timing.

• • • •

BY THE END OF THIS chapter, readers will understand how to implement robust BLE communication in their Rust-based embedded systems. We've seen how Rust's safety features and performance characteristics make it particularly well-suited for implementing reliable wireless communications. The combination of BLE's power efficiency with Rust's strong guarantees creates a powerful platform for developing modern wireless embedded applications.

• • • •

OUR EXPLORATION OF BLE programming demonstrates that Rust provides an excellent foundation for implementing wireless communication in embedded systems. Whether creating IoT devices, sensor networks, or control systems, Rust's safety guarantees and performance characteristics make it an ideal choice for BLE development, ensuring reliable and efficient wireless communication while preventing common programming errors.

32. WiFi Communication in Rust

WiFi connectivity has become a cornerstone of modern embedded systems, enabling devices to communicate over IP networks and integrate with cloud services. This chapter explores implementing robust WiFi communication in Rust, focusing on creating reliable network connections while maintaining security and efficiency in resource-constrained environments.

• • • •

AT THE HEART OF WIFI implementation lies the challenge of managing network states and connections. Using Rust's embedded-hal and network interface abstractions, we'll implement WiFi functionality that handles connection establishment, maintenance, and recovery gracefully. The esp-wifi crate serves as our primary tool for WiFi operations, providing a safe interface to the underlying hardware while maintaining Rust's safety guarantees.

• • • •

NETWORK CONFIGURATION presents numerous challenges in embedded systems. We'll explore implementing both static and dynamic IP configuration, DNS resolution, and network parameter management. Rust's type system helps prevent common networking errors while ensuring proper handling of configuration parameters. We'll implement methods for storing network credentials securely and managing multiple network profiles for different environments.

• • • •

ERROR RESILIENCE BECOMES crucial in wireless communications. We'll implement comprehensive error handling for various network scenarios - connection drops, weak signals, interference, and authentication failures. Rust's Result type proves invaluable here, allowing us to create robust error recovery mechanisms while maintaining code clarity. Our implementation includes automatic reconnection strategies and fallback mechanisms for maintaining network connectivity.

• • • •

SECURITY IN WIFI COMMUNICATIONS requires careful consideration. We'll implement proper encryption handling for various security protocols (WPA2, WPA3), certificate management, and secure storage of network credentials. Rust's security features help prevent common vulnerabilities while implementing these protocols. We'll also explore implementing secure communication layers above the WiFi connection, including TLS for application-level security.

• • • •

POWER MANAGEMENT PLAYS a vital role in WiFi-enabled embedded systems. We'll examine implementing power-saving modes, managing sleep states, and optimizing transmission patterns to extend battery life. This includes implementing proper wake-up mechanisms for periodic network operations while maintaining low power consumption during idle periods. Rust's zero-cost abstractions ensure our power management code remains efficient while being maintainable.

• • • •

NETWORK STACK IMPLEMENTATION requires careful attention to resource usage. We'll explore implementing TCP/IP communications efficiently, managing socket connections, and handling network buffers appropriately. Rust's ownership model helps prevent common networking bugs like buffer overflows and memory leaks while maintaining high performance. We'll implement both TCP and UDP communications, showing appropriate use cases for each protocol.

• • • •

MQTT AND HTTP IMPLEMENTATIONS often form the backbone of IoT communications. We'll create robust implementations of these protocols over our WiFi connection, focusing on reliable message delivery and efficient resource usage. This includes implementing proper QoS levels for MQTT and handling HTTP requests efficiently. Rust's async/await syntax helps manage these concurrent operations clearly and safely.

• • • •

PERFORMANCE OPTIMIZATION in WiFi communications involves careful balancing of throughput and resource usage. We'll explore techniques for optimizing data transmission, including proper packet sizing, buffer management, and transmission timing. We'll implement these optimizations while maintaining type safety and preventing common programming errors that could affect network performance.

• • • •

REAL-WORLD WIFI IMPLEMENTATIONS must handle various network environments and conditions. We'll implement adaptive behavior for different network qualities, including handling varying signal strengths, network congestion, and changing environmental conditions. This includes implementing proper metrics collection for network quality and adjusting communication patterns accordingly.

• • • •

TESTING WIFI IMPLEMENTATIONS presents unique challenges. We'll develop comprehensive testing strategies that include unit testing for protocol handling, integration testing with real networks, and simulation-based testing for various network conditions. This includes creating mock network interfaces for testing and implementing proper test coverage for network operations.

• • • •

INTEROPERABILITY WITH existing network infrastructure requires careful consideration. We'll explore implementing standard network protocols and services while maintaining compatibility with various network configurations. This includes handling different WiFi standards, implementing proper service discovery, and managing network address translation (NAT) scenarios.

• • • •

BY THE END OF THIS chapter, readers will understand how to implement reliable WiFi communication in their Rust-based embedded systems. We've seen how Rust's safety features and performance characteristics make it particularly well-suited for implementing robust network communications. The combination of WiFi connectivity with Rust's strong guarantees creates a powerful platform for developing connected embedded applications.

• • • •

THIS EXPLORATION OF WiFi programming demonstrates that Rust provides an excellent foundation for implementing network communication in embedded systems. Whether creating IoT devices, networked sensors, or control systems, Rust's safety guarantees and performance characteristics make it an ideal choice for WiFi development, ensuring reliable and efficient network communication while preventing common programming errors.

33. Security Best Practices for IoT

Security is paramount when developing IoT devices and embedded systems, as these devices often handle sensitive data and can become targets for malicious actors. In this chapter, we will explore comprehensive security best practices that should be implemented when developing IoT devices using Rust, ensuring that our systems remain resilient against various forms of attacks while maintaining functionality and performance.

One of the fundamental aspects of IoT security is the principle of defense in depth. This approach involves implementing multiple layers of security controls to protect the system, ensuring that if one layer is compromised, others remain intact to maintain overall system security. When developing IoT devices with Rust, we can leverage the language's inherent safety features while adding additional security measures.

Authentication and authorization form the cornerstone of IoT security. Every device in an IoT network should implement robust authentication mechanisms to verify the identity of users, other devices, and services attempting to interact with it. Rust's strong type system and ownership model help prevent common security vulnerabilities, but we must still implement proper authentication protocols. JSON Web Tokens (JWT) are commonly used for this purpose, and Rust provides excellent libraries such as jsonwebtoken for implementing JWT-based authentication.

Data encryption is another critical aspect of IoT security. All sensitive data, whether at rest or in transit, should be encrypted using strong cryptographic algorithms. Rust's ecosystem offers several cryptography libraries, with ring being one of the most popular choices. When implementing encryption, it's essential to use well-vetted algorithms and avoid implementing custom cryptographic solutions. Always encrypt sensitive configuration data, user credentials, and any personally identifiable information (PII) stored on the device.

Secure communication protocols are essential for IoT devices that communicate over networks. Always use encrypted protocols such as HTTPS, MQTT over TLS, or other secure variants of common protocols. Rust's native-tls and openssl crates provide the necessary tools to implement secure communication channels. Additionally, implement certificate validation and pinning to prevent man-in-the-middle attacks.

Regular security updates are crucial for maintaining the security of IoT devices throughout their lifecycle. Implement a secure over-the-air (OTA) update mechanism that verifies the authenticity and integrity of firmware updates before applying them. This involves implementing digital signature verification and ensuring that the update process cannot be interrupted or corrupted. The update mechanism should also include rollback capabilities in case of failed updates.

Access control and privilege management are essential security considerations. Implement the principle of least privilege, ensuring that processes and users only have access to the resources they absolutely need. Rust's ownership system helps enforce access control at the code level, but we must also implement proper system-level access controls. This includes securing debug interfaces, disabling unnecessary services, and implementing proper file system permissions.

Network security is particularly important for IoT devices. Implement proper network segmentation, ensuring that devices can only communicate with necessary services and other devices. Use firewalls and network filtering to restrict unnecessary traffic. When possible, implement network intrusion detection systems (IDS) to monitor for suspicious activity. Always disable unnecessary network services and ports.

Secure boot mechanisms ensure that only authorized firmware can run on the device. Implement secure boot by verifying digital signatures of firmware images before execution. This prevents unauthorized or malicious firmware from being loaded onto the device. The bootloader should be protected and immutable, forming the root of trust for the system.

Input validation is crucial for preventing various types of attacks. Always validate and sanitize all input data, whether it comes from users, other devices, or network sources. Rust's strong type system helps prevent many common input-related vulnerabilities, but we must still implement proper validation logic for application-specific requirements.

Logging and monitoring are essential for security purposes. Implement secure logging mechanisms that record security-relevant events while protecting the confidentiality of sensitive information. Ensure that logs cannot be tampered with and implement proper log rotation to prevent storage exhaustion attacks. Consider implementing remote logging to a secure server for better audit capabilities.

Physical security should not be overlooked. Implement tamper detection mechanisms where possible, and ensure that sensitive information cannot be extracted from the device through physical access. This includes protecting debug interfaces, securing storage media, and implementing proper key storage mechanisms.

Error handling in security-critical code requires special attention. Implement proper error handling that doesn't leak sensitive information through error messages. Use Rust's Result type to handle errors gracefully and ensure that the system fails securely when errors occur.

Resource management is crucial for preventing denial-of-service attacks. Implement proper resource limits and monitoring to prevent resource exhaustion. This includes managing memory allocation, file handles, network connections, and other system resources. Rust's ownership system helps prevent memory-related vulnerabilities, but we must still implement proper resource management at the application level.

Security testing should be an integral part of the development process. Implement automated security testing as part of the continuous integration pipeline. This includes static analysis, dependency checking, and vulnerability scanning. Regular penetration testing should also be performed to identify potential security weaknesses.

Documentation of security features and configurations is essential for maintaining security throughout the device's lifecycle. Maintain detailed documentation of all security mechanisms, including configuration requirements, update procedures, and incident response plans. This documentation should be kept up to date and accessible to relevant team members.

Finally, implement proper security incident response procedures. This includes mechanisms for detecting security incidents, procedures for responding to incidents, and plans for recovering from security breaches. The incident response plan should be tested regularly to ensure its effectiveness.

Remember that security is an ongoing process, not a one-time implementation. Regularly review and update security measures as new threats emerge and vulnerabilities are discovered. Stay informed about security best practices and emerging threats in the IoT security landscape. Participate in security communities and share knowledge about security challenges and solutions in the embedded Rust ecosystem.

By following these security best practices and implementing them properly in our Rust-based IoT devices, we can create more resilient and secure systems that protect both the devices and their users from potential security threats. The next chapter will dive deeper into specific cryptography implementations that can be used to enhance the security of our IoT devices.

34. Cryptography Implementation

Chapter 34: Cryptography Implementation

Implementing robust cryptography is essential for securing embedded systems and IoT devices. In this chapter, we'll explore practical implementations of cryptographic algorithms and protocols using Rust, focusing on solutions that are suitable for resource-constrained environments while maintaining strong security guarantees.

The foundation of cryptographic implementations in Rust typically begins with choosing appropriate cryptographic libraries. The ring crate stands out as a popular choice for embedded systems due to its focus on safe, efficient implementations of common cryptographic primitives. For more specialized needs, the RustCrypto suite of crates provides modular implementations of various algorithms. Let's examine how to implement essential cryptographic operations using these tools.

Symmetric encryption forms the backbone of many security implementations in embedded systems. AES (Advanced Encryption Standard) remains the most widely used symmetric encryption algorithm, with AES-256 being the recommended variant for most applications. Here's how we might implement AES encryption in Rust using the aes-gcm crate:

```rust
use aes_gcm::{Aes256Gcm, Key, Nonce};
use aes_gcm::aead::{Aead, NewAead};
fn encrypt_data(key: &[u8; 32], nonce: &[u8; 12], plaintext: &[u8]) -> Vec<u8> {
let cipher = Aes256Gcm::new(Key::from_slice(key));
let nonce = Nonce::from_slice(nonce);
cipher.encrypt(nonce, plaintext).expect("encryption failure!")
}
```

When implementing symmetric encryption, proper key management is crucial. Never store encryption keys directly in the firmware or in easily accessible locations. Consider using a hardware security module (HSM) or trusted platform module (TPM) when available. For systems without hardware security features, implement secure key derivation functions (KDF) to generate encryption keys from master keys or passwords.

Public key cryptography is essential for secure communication and digital signatures. The RSA algorithm, while widely used, can be computationally expensive for embedded systems. Elliptic Curve Cryptography (ECC) provides a more efficient alternative while maintaining strong security. The p256 crate implements the NIST P-256 curve, which is suitable for most embedded applications:

```rust
use p256::SecretKey;
use p256::ecdsa::{SigningKey, Signature, signature::Signer};
fn generate_signature(message: &[u8], secret_key: &SecretKey)
-> Signature {
let signing_key = SigningKey::from(secret_key);
signing_key.sign(message)
}
```

Hash functions are fundamental cryptographic primitives used in many security applications. The SHA-2 and SHA-3 families of hash functions are currently recommended for cryptographic use. When implementing hashing in embedded systems, consider the trade-off between security and performance. SHA-256 provides a good balance for most applications:

```rust
use sha2::{Sha256, Digest};
fn compute_hash(data: &[u8]) -> [u8; 32] {
```

```
let mut hasher = Sha256::new();
hasher.update(data);
hasher.finalize().into()
}
```

Random number generation is critical for many cryptographic operations. In embedded systems, implementing proper random number generation can be challenging due to limited entropy sources. The rand crate provides a good foundation, but you should ensure proper seeding from hardware entropy sources when available:

```rust
use rand::{RngCore, SeedableRng};
use rand_chacha::ChaCha20Rng;
fn generate_random_bytes(len: usize) -> Vec<u8> {
let mut rng = ChaCha20Rng::from_entropy();
let mut bytes = vec![0u8; len];
rng.fill_bytes(&mut bytes);
bytes
}
```

Message authentication codes (MACs) and authenticated encryption are essential for ensuring data integrity and authenticity. The HMAC algorithm, combined with a strong hash function, provides a reliable way to implement message authentication:

```rust
use hmac::{Hmac, Mac};
use sha2::Sha256;
fn compute_hmac(key: &[u8], message: &[u8]) -> [u8; 32] {
type HmacSha256 = Hmac<Sha256>;
let mut mac = HmacSha256::new_from_slice(key).expect("HMAC init failed");
```

```
mac.update(message);
mac.finalize().into_bytes().into()
}
```

When implementing cryptographic operations in embedded systems, consider the performance implications. Some operations, particularly public key cryptography, can be computationally expensive. Implement caching mechanisms where appropriate, but be careful not to introduce security vulnerabilities through the cache implementation.

Error handling in cryptographic operations requires special attention. Cryptographic errors should never reveal sensitive information through error messages or timing differences. Implement proper error handling that maintains security while providing useful debugging information:

```rust
use thiserror::Error;
#[derive(Error, Debug)]
enum CryptoError {
#[error("Encryption failed")]
EncryptionError,
#[error("Decryption failed")]
DecryptionError,
#[error("Invalid key length")]
KeyLengthError,
}
```

Side-channel attacks pose a particular risk to embedded systems. Implement constant-time operations for cryptographic functions to prevent timing attacks. The subtle crate provides tools for implementing constant-time operations:

```rust
```

```
use subtle::ConstantTimeEq;
fn constant_time_compare(a: &[u8], b: &[u8]) -> bool {
if a.len() != b.len() {
return false;
}
a.ct_eq(b).into()
}
```

Key rotation and management are essential aspects of cryptographic implementations. Implement proper key rotation mechanisms and ensure that old keys can be securely deleted when no longer needed. Consider implementing forward secrecy where appropriate to limit the impact of key compromises.

Testing cryptographic implementations requires special consideration. Include tests for known test vectors, edge cases, and error conditions. Implement fuzz testing to identify potential vulnerabilities:

```rust
#[cfg(test)]
mod tests {
use super::*;
#[test]
fn test_encryption_decryption() {
let key = [0u8; 32];
let nonce = [0u8; 12];
let plaintext = b"test message";
let ciphertext = encrypt_data(&key, &nonce, plaintext);
// Add decryption and verification
}
}
```

Remember that implementing cryptography correctly is challenging, and small mistakes can lead to significant vulnerabilities. Always prefer well-tested, widely-used cryptographic libraries over custom implementations. Keep up with current cryptographic standards and best practices, and be prepared to update implementations as new vulnerabilities are discovered and new algorithms are recommended.

The next chapter will build upon these cryptographic foundations to implement secure boot and update mechanisms for embedded systems, ensuring the integrity and authenticity of firmware throughout the device lifecycle.

35. Secure Boot and Updates

Chapter 35 focuses on implementing secure boot and update mechanisms for embedded systems, building upon the cryptographic foundations established in the previous chapter.

Secure boot and update mechanisms are critical components of a robust embedded system security architecture. They ensure that only authorized and verified code runs on the device, protecting against malicious code injection and unauthorized modifications. Let's explore how to implement these security features using Rust.

A secure boot process typically begins with a hardware root of trust, often provided by the microcontroller's boot ROM or secure element. This immutable code verifies the first stage bootloader, which then verifies subsequent stages until the main application is loaded. Here's how we might implement a bootloader verification function:

```rust
use sha2::{Sha256, Digest};
use ed25519_dalek::{PublicKey, Signature, Verifier};
struct BootloaderStage {
code: Vec<u8>,
signature: [u8; 64],
next_stage_public_key: Option<[u8; 32]>,
}
fn verify_bootloader_stage(stage: &BootloaderStage, public_key: &PublicKey) -> bool {
let signature = Signature::from_bytes(&stage.signature)
.expect("Invalid signature format");
let message = compute_stage_hash(&stage.code);
public_key.verify(&message, &signature).is_ok()
}
```

The boot sequence should implement a chain of trust, where each stage verifies the next before transferring control. This verification typically includes checking cryptographic signatures and hash values. It's important to store verification keys securely, preferably in hardware security elements or protected storage regions.

Secure updates are equally important, enabling devices to receive security patches and feature updates while preventing unauthorized modifications. A robust update system should implement version control, rollback protection, and atomic updates. Here's an example of an update package structure:

```rust
struct UpdatePackage {
version: u32,
target_hardware_id: u32,
payload: Vec<u8>,
signature: [u8; 64],
metadata: UpdateMetadata,
}
struct UpdateMetadata {
minimum_compatible_version: u32,
release_date: u64,
critical_update: bool,
}
impl UpdatePackage {
fn verify(&self, public_key: &PublicKey) -> Result<(), UpdateError> {
// Verify signature
let signature = Signature::from_bytes(&self.signature)?;
let message = self.compute_payload_hash();
public_key.verify(&message, &signature)?;
// Verify hardware compatibility
```

```
if self.target_hardware_id != get_hardware_id() {
return Err(UpdateError::IncompatibleHardware);
}
// Check version constraints
if self.version <= get_current_version() {
return Err(UpdateError::VersionDowngrade);
}
Ok(())
}
}
```

Implementing atomic updates is crucial to prevent devices from entering an inconsistent state if the update process is interrupted. One common approach is to maintain two firmware slots: active and backup. Here's a simplified implementation of a dual-bank update system:

```rust
struct FirmwareBank {
base_address: u32,
size: u32,
version: u32,
status: BankStatus,
}
enum BankStatus {
Empty,
Valid,
Active,
Invalid,
}
struct DualBankUpdater {
bank_a: FirmwareBank,
bank_b: FirmwareBank,
```

```
}
impl DualBankUpdater {
fn apply_update(&mut self, package: UpdatePackage) -> Result<(), UpdateError> {
let target_bank = self.get_inactive_bank()?;
// Write new firmware to inactive bank
self.write_firmware(target_bank, &package.payload)?;
// Verify written firmware
if !self.verify_firmware(target_bank) {
return Err(UpdateError::VerificationFailed);
}
// Update bank status
self.switch_active_bank(target_bank)?;
Ok(())
}
}
```

Rollback protection is essential to prevent attackers from downgrading firmware to versions with known vulnerabilities. Implement a monotonic counter or similar mechanism to track version numbers:

```rust
use embedded_hal::nvmem::NvMem;
struct VersionCounter {
storage: Box<dyn NvMem>,
current_version: u32,
}
impl VersionCounter {
fn update_version(&mut self, new_version: u32) -> Result<(), UpdateError> {
if new_version <= self.current_version {
return Err(UpdateError::VersionDowngrade);
```

```
}
self.storage.write(0, &new_version.to_le_bytes())?;
self.current_version = new_version;
Ok(())
}
}
```

Error handling during the update process requires special attention. The system should be able to recover from power failures or other interruptions without becoming unusable:

```rust
fn perform_update(package: UpdatePackage) -> Result<(), UpdateError> {
// Verify update package before starting
package.verify(&get_public_key())?;
// Save recovery information
save_recovery_state(RecoveryState::UpdateStarted)?;
// Apply update
apply_update_package(&package)?;
// Verify new firmware
verify_installed_firmware()?;
// Update version counter
update_version_counter(package.version)?;
// Clear recovery state
clear_recovery_state()?;
Ok(())
}
```

Testing secure boot and update implementations requires thorough validation across various scenarios:

```rust
#[cfg(test)]
```

```
mod tests {
use super::*;
#[test]
fn test_update_verification() {
let package = create_test_update_package();
let result = package.verify(&TEST_PUBLIC_KEY);
assert!(result.is_ok());
}
#[test]
fn test_rollback_protection() {
let mut counter = VersionCounter::new();
assert!(counter.update_version(2).is_ok());
assert!(counter.update_version(1).is_err());
}
}
```

Secure logging of boot and update events is important for debugging and audit purposes. Implement a secure logging mechanism that records critical events while protecting log integrity:

```rust
struct SecureLogger {
storage: Box<dyn NvMem>,
hmac_key: [u8; 32],
}
impl SecureLogger {
fn log_event(&mut self, event: BootEvent) -> Result<(), LogError> {
let timestamp = get_timestamp();
let entry = LogEntry {
timestamp,
event,
sequence_number: self.get_next_sequence(),
```

```
};
let hmac = compute_entry_hmac(&entry, &self.hmac_key);
self.write_log_entry(&entry, &hmac)?;
Ok(())
}
}
```

Remember that secure boot and update mechanisms are critical security features that must be thoroughly tested and regularly audited. Keep the implementation as simple as possible while maintaining strong security guarantees, and always plan for failure scenarios and recovery procedures.

36. Resource Constrained Programming

Let's explore the critical aspects of programming for resource constrained environments, a fundamental skill for embedded systems developers working with devices that have limited memory, processing power, and energy resources.

Resource constrained programming in embedded Rust requires a deep understanding of both hardware limitations and software optimization techniques. When working with microcontrollers that might have only a few kilobytes of RAM and limited flash storage, every byte counts, and efficient code becomes paramount.

Memory management is perhaps the most critical aspect of resource constrained programming. Rust's zero cost abstractions help tremendously here, as they provide high level programming constructs without runtime overhead. Let's look at some techniques for minimizing memory usage:

```rust
// Instead of using Vec<T>, use fixed size arrays when possible
const MAX_ITEMS: usize = 16;
struct BufferManager {
data: [u8; MAX_ITEMS],
length: usize,
}
// Use static allocation instead of dynamic allocation
static mut GLOBAL_BUFFER: [u8; 1024] = [0; 1024];
// Leverage Rust's const generics for compile time memory management
struct RingBuffer<const N: usize> {
data: [u8; N],
read_index: usize,
write_index: usize,
}
```

```

Stack usage is another crucial consideration. Deep call chains can quickly exhaust the limited stack space available on microcontrollers. We can use static analysis tools to help track stack usage:

```rust
#[inline(never)]
fn deep_function() {
// Using attribute to prevent inlining helps with stack analysis
let buffer = [0u8; 512]; // Large stack allocation
process_data(&buffer);
}
// Use const fn for compile time computation
const fn calculate_buffer_size(width: usize, height: usize) -> usize {
width * height
}
```

Flash memory constraints require careful consideration of code size. Rust's powerful type system and zero cost abstractions help write compact code without sacrificing safety or readability:

```rust
// Use the #[inline] attribute judiciously
#[inline(always)]
fn critical_timing_function() {
// Time sensitive operations
}
// Leverage const fn for compile time computation
const fn lookup_table() -> [u8; 256] {
let mut table = [0u8; 256];
let mut i = 0;
while i < 256 {
```
```

```
table[i] = compute_value(i);
i += 1;
}
table
}
```

When working with limited processing power, efficient algorithms become crucial. Consider using lookup tables instead of complex calculations, especially for frequently used operations:

```rust
// Precomputed sine table for fast trigonometry
static SINE_TABLE: [i16; 360] = generate_sine_table();
fn fast_sine(angle: u16) -> i16 {
SINE_TABLE[angle as usize % 360]
}
// Bit manipulation instead of division
fn divide_by_power_of_two(value: u32, power: u8) -> u32 {
value >> power
}
```

Resource constrained systems often need to handle multiple tasks with limited resources. Here's an example of a simple task scheduler that uses minimal memory:

```rust
struct Task {
priority: u8,
interval: u32,
last_run: u32,
function: fn(),
}
struct Scheduler {
tasks: [Option<Task>; 8],
```

```
current_time: u32,
}
impl Scheduler {
fn run(&mut self) {
loop {
for task in self.tasks.iter_mut().flatten() {
if self.current_time - task.last_run >= task.interval {
(task.function)();
task.last_run = self.current_time;
}
}
self.current_time = self.current_time.wrapping_add(1);
}
}
}
```

Power consumption is often a critical constraint in embedded systems. Here's an example of power aware programming:

```rust
enum PowerMode {
Active,
Sleep,
DeepSleep,
}
struct PowerManager {
current_mode: PowerMode,
peripherals: u32,
}
impl PowerManager {
fn enter_sleep_mode(&mut self) {
// Disable unnecessary peripherals
self.disable_unused_peripherals();
```

```
// Configure wake up sources
self.configure_wake_sources();
// Enter sleep mode
cortex_m::asm::wfi();
}
}
```

Error handling in resource constrained environments requires careful consideration. Traditional Result and Option types might be too costly in terms of memory usage. Consider using compact error handling approaches:

```rust
// Use smaller error types
#[derive(Debug)]
struct CompactError(u8);
// Implement custom error handling without allocation
fn fallible_operation() -> Result<(), CompactError> {
if some_condition() {
Ok(())
} else {
Err(CompactError(1))
}
}
```

Debugging support in resource constrained environments often requires creative solutions. Here's an example of a minimal logging system:

```rust
struct RingLogger {
buffer: [u8; 64],
position: usize,
}
```

```
impl RingLogger {
fn log(&mut self, message: &[u8]) {
for &byte in message {
self.buffer[self.position] = byte;
self.position = (self.position + 1) % self.buffer.len();
}
}
}
```

Remember that resource constraints often require tradeoffs. The key is to make these tradeoffs explicit and document the reasoning behind them. Always measure and profile your code to ensure it meets the system's constraints:

```rust
#[cfg(feature = "profiling")]
pub fn profile_critical_section() {
let start = cycle_count();
critical_operation();
let end = cycle_count();
log_cycles(end - start);
}
```

Resource constrained programming is as much about understanding your system's limitations as it is about writing efficient code. Always consider the impact of your design decisions on memory usage, processing requirements, and power consumption. Use Rust's powerful type system and zero cost abstractions to write efficient, safe code that runs reliably on constrained hardware.

37. Power Management Techniques

Power management stands as a critical component in modern embedded systems, often determining the practical viability of battery-powered devices and energy-efficient applications. This chapter explores implementing sophisticated power management strategies in Rust, leveraging the language's precision and safety features to create efficient, reliable power control systems.

• • • •

EFFECTIVE POWER MANAGEMENT begins with understanding the various power states available in embedded systems. We'll examine implementing sleep modes, ranging from light sleep states that maintain some peripherals active to deep sleep modes that shut down most system functions. Rust's type system helps ensure that transitions between these states happen safely, preventing common errors that could lead to unexpected power consumption or system instability.

• • • •

DYNAMIC FREQUENCY SCALING represents a powerful technique for managing processor power consumption. We'll explore implementing adaptive clock frequency management, adjusting system speed based on computational demands. This includes creating safe abstractions for clock control, managing peripheral timing dependencies, and ensuring smooth transitions between frequency states. Rust's zero-cost abstractions allow us to implement these features without adding runtime overhead.

• • • •

PERIPHERAL POWER MANAGEMENT requires careful orchestration of device states. We'll implement strategies for selectively enabling and disabling peripherals based on system needs, managing power domains, and handling device wake-up sequences. Our implementation includes proper state tracking to prevent accessing disabled peripherals and ensure efficient power usage across all system components.

• • • •

BATTERY MANAGEMENT presents unique challenges in embedded systems. We'll explore implementing battery monitoring systems, including voltage tracking, charge state estimation, and load management. This includes creating safe abstractions for ADC readings, implementing proper scaling and calibration, and managing system behavior based on battery status. Rust's strong typing helps prevent common errors in voltage calculations and state management.

• • • •

EVENT-DRIVEN POWER management allows systems to respond efficiently to varying workloads. We'll implement event detection and handling mechanisms that trigger appropriate power state transitions. This includes managing interrupt-driven wake-up sources, handling timeout-based state changes, and implementing power-aware task scheduling. Rust's ownership model helps prevent race conditions and ensure proper synchronization in these event-driven scenarios.

• • • •

TEMPERATURE MANAGEMENT often intertwines with power control. We'll explore implementing thermal monitoring and management systems, including temperature-based frequency scaling and thermal protection mechanisms. This includes creating safe interfaces for temperature sensors, implementing proper threshold management, and ensuring system stability across temperature ranges.

• • • •

COMMUNICATION INTERFACES often contribute significantly to power consumption. We'll implement power-aware communication strategies, including duty-cycling radio interfaces, managing transmission power levels, and optimizing protocol timing. This includes implementing proper power state transitions for wireless interfaces and ensuring efficient message buffering and transmission scheduling.

• • • •

SENSOR POWER MANAGEMENT requires balancing measurement accuracy with energy efficiency. We'll explore implementing adaptive sampling rates, sensor sleep modes, and efficient data collection strategies. This includes managing sensor warm-up times, implementing proper calibration sequences, and ensuring data validity across power state transitions.

• • • •

REAL-TIME CONSTRAINTS must be maintained while managing power consumption. We'll implement power-aware real-time scheduling, ensuring critical tasks meet their deadlines while minimizing energy usage. This includes managing timer peripherals efficiently, implementing proper wake-up mechanisms, and ensuring predictable system response times across power states.

• • • •

ERROR HANDLING BECOMES particularly important in power management systems. We'll implement robust error detection and recovery mechanisms for power-related failures, including brown-out detection, voltage monitoring, and safe system shutdown procedures. Rust's error handling patterns help create reliable recovery procedures while maintaining system stability.

• • • •

TESTING POWER MANAGEMENT implementations requires specialized approaches. We'll develop testing strategies that include power consumption measurement, state transition verification, and long-term stability testing. This includes creating test fixtures for power monitoring, implementing power profiling tools, and ensuring proper test coverage for power-related functionality.

• • • •

MEMORY MANAGEMENT INTERACTS significantly with power consumption. We'll explore implementing power-aware memory management strategies, including proper use of retention RAM, managing flash memory operations, and optimizing memory access patterns. This includes implementing efficient data structures that minimize power-consuming memory operations.

• • • •

BY THE END OF THIS chapter, readers will understand how to implement comprehensive power management in their Rust-based embedded systems. We've seen how Rust's safety features and performance characteristics make it particularly well-suited for implementing reliable power control systems. The combination of efficient power management with Rust's strong guarantees creates a robust foundation for developing long-lasting, energy-efficient embedded applications.

• • • •

THIS EXPLORATION OF power management techniques demonstrates that Rust provides an excellent foundation for implementing sophisticated power control systems. Whether creating battery-powered devices, energy-harvesting systems, or power-aware applications, Rust's safety guarantees and performance characteristics make it an ideal choice for power management development, ensuring reliable and efficient operation while preventing common programming errors.

38. Real-Time Systems Design

Real-time systems represent a critical domain in embedded development where timing guarantees and predictable behavior are paramount. This chapter explores implementing real-time systems in Rust, demonstrating how the language's zero-cost abstractions and safety features can be leveraged to create deterministic, reliable systems that meet strict timing requirements.

• • • •

AT THE CORE OF REAL-time system design lies the concept of deterministic timing. We'll explore how Rust's static memory management and zero-cost abstractions enable us to create systems with predictable execution times. Unlike garbage-collected languages that can introduce unpredictable pauses, Rust's ownership model allows us to reason about timing behavior at compile time, making it particularly suitable for hard real-time systems.

• • • •

TASK SCHEDULING FORMS the foundation of real-time systems. We'll examine implementing both fixed-priority and deadline-driven scheduling algorithms in Rust. The implementation includes priority inheritance mechanisms to prevent priority inversion, deadline monitoring, and proper handling of task overruns. Rust's type system helps ensure that task priorities and deadlines are properly enforced, preventing common scheduling errors at compile time.

• • • •

INTERRUPT HANDLING in real-time systems requires careful attention to latency and determinism. We'll explore implementing interrupt handlers that maintain predictable response times while ensuring system stability. This includes proper interrupt prioritization, nested interrupt handling, and techniques for minimizing interrupt latency. Rust's unsafe blocks are carefully contained within safe abstractions to maintain system integrity while allowing low-level interrupt manipulation.

• • • •

RESOURCE MANAGEMENT becomes particularly critical in real-time systems. We'll implement deterministic resource allocation strategies, including priority ceiling and priority inheritance protocols to prevent priority inversion. Rust's ownership system naturally maps to these resource management patterns, helping prevent deadlocks and ensuring proper resource release even in error conditions.

• • • •

TIMING ANALYSIS FORMS a crucial part of real-time system design. We'll explore implementing timing measurement and analysis tools, including worst-case execution time (WCET) analysis and deadline monitoring. This includes creating instrumentation points that don't affect system timing, implementing proper timestamp handling, and ensuring accurate timing measurements across different system states.

• • • •

MEMORY MANAGEMENT IN real-time systems must be predictable and deterministic. We'll examine implementing static memory allocation strategies, memory pools for dynamic allocation needs, and techniques for preventing memory fragmentation. Rust's compile-time memory management helps ensure that our memory usage remains predictable while preventing common memory-related errors.

• • • •

INTER-TASK COMMUNICATION in real-time systems requires careful consideration of timing behavior. We'll implement deterministic communication mechanisms, including message queues with priority inheritance, bounded priority inversion, and predictable synchronization primitives. Rust's type system helps ensure that communication patterns maintain the required timing properties while preventing race conditions.

• • • •

ERROR HANDLING IN REAL-time systems must maintain timing guarantees even during fault conditions. We'll explore implementing fault detection and recovery mechanisms that operate within predictable time bounds. This includes implementing watchdog timers, handling task timeouts, and ensuring proper system recovery without violating timing constraints.

• • • •

PERIODIC TASK MANAGEMENT forms a common pattern in real-time systems. We'll implement mechanisms for handling periodic tasks with different frequencies, including proper phase management and jitter control. This includes implementing efficient timer management, handling timer overruns, and ensuring proper task scheduling across different periodic boundaries.

• • • •

MODE CHANGES IN REAL-time systems require careful handling to maintain timing guarantees during transitions. We'll explore implementing mode change protocols that ensure predictable behavior during system reconfiguration. This includes managing task sets across mode changes, handling timing requirements during transitions, and ensuring system stability during reconfiguration.

• • • •

SYSTEM INITIALIZATION in real-time applications requires special attention. We'll implement deterministic startup sequences that establish proper system state while maintaining timing guarantees. This includes implementing proper peripheral initialization, task creation, and system state verification within bounded time limits.

• • • •

TESTING REAL-TIME SYSTEMS presents unique challenges. We'll develop specialized testing approaches that verify timing behavior, including response time analysis, deadline verification, and long-term stability testing. This includes creating test harnesses that can verify timing properties without affecting system behavior.

• • • •

BY THE END OF THIS chapter, readers will understand how to implement reliable real-time systems using Rust. We've seen how Rust's safety features and performance characteristics make it particularly well-suited for real-time application development. The combination of deterministic behavior with Rust's strong guarantees creates a powerful platform for developing critical real-time systems.

• • • •

THIS EXPLORATION OF real-time systems design demonstrates that Rust provides an excellent foundation for implementing time-critical applications. Whether creating industrial control systems, automotive applications, or other time-sensitive systems, Rust's safety guarantees and performance characteristics make it an ideal choice for real-time development, ensuring reliable and predictable operation while preventing common programming errors.

39. RTOS Implementation in Rust

Real Time Operating Systems (RTOS) play a crucial role in embedded systems where timing, task management, and resource sharing are critical. In this chapter, we'll explore how to implement an RTOS using Rust, leveraging the language's safety features while maintaining the performance requirements of real time systems.

At its core, an RTOS implementation in Rust requires careful consideration of several key components: task scheduling, context switching, interrupt handling, and resource management. Let's begin by examining how we can implement a basic task scheduler. In Rust, we can represent tasks as closures or functions that can be executed by our scheduler. The scheduler needs to maintain a queue of tasks and determine which task should run next based on priority levels and timing constraints.

Here's how we might implement a basic task structure:

```rust
pub struct Task {
priority: u8,
stack_pointer: *mut u8,
state: TaskState,
context: Context,
}
```

The context switching mechanism is one of the most critical parts of an RTOS implementation. In Rust, we need to be particularly careful about ownership and borrowing rules when switching between tasks. We can implement context switching using unsafe blocks where necessary, but we'll wrap these unsafe operations in safe abstractions to maintain Rust's safety guarantees wherever possible.

Memory management in an RTOS context requires special attention. Rust's ownership model helps prevent common memory-related bugs, but we need to carefully design our memory allocation strategy. Many embedded RTOS implementations use a fixed-size memory pool to avoid heap fragmentation. We can implement this in Rust using a static array and a custom allocator:

```rust
pub struct MemoryPool {
pool: [u8; POOL_SIZE],
allocation_table: [bool; BLOCK_COUNT],
}
```

Priority-based scheduling is another essential component of an RTOS. We can implement a priority queue using Rust's standard collections or create our own lock-free implementation for better performance. The scheduler needs to ensure that higher-priority tasks can preempt lower-priority ones while maintaining system stability.

Interprocess communication (IPC) mechanisms are crucial for any RTOS. In Rust, we can implement message queues, semaphores, and mutexes using the language's synchronization primitives. For example, a basic message queue might look like this:

```rust
pub struct MessageQueue<T> {
buffer: Ring<T>,
waiting_tasks: Queue<TaskId>,
}
```

Time management is another critical aspect of RTOS implementation. We need to handle both periodic tasks and deadline-based scheduling. Rust's type system can help us enforce timing constraints at compile time:

```rust
pub struct Deadline {
absolute_time: Instant,
task_id: TaskId,
}
```

Error handling in an RTOS context requires careful consideration. Rust's Result and Option types provide excellent tools for handling errors without runtime overhead. We can define custom error types for different subsystems:

```rust
pub enum RTOSError {
TaskCreationFailed,
SchedulerOverflow,
DeadlineMissed,
ResourceUnavailable,
}
```

Real time constraints require careful attention to interrupt handling. We can use Rust's #[interrupt] attribute and the cortex_m crate to implement interrupt handlers that integrate with our scheduler:

```rust
#[interrupt]
fn SysTick() {
critical_section::with(|_| {
SCHEDULER.tick();
check_deadlines();
});
}
```

Resource management in an RTOS requires careful consideration of priority inheritance to prevent priority inversion. We can implement this using Rust's type system to track resource ownership and adjust task priorities dynamically:

```rust
pub struct Mutex<T> {
data: UnsafeCell<T>,
owner: Option<TaskId>,
original_priority: Option<u8>,
}
```

Testing an RTOS implementation requires both unit tests and integration tests. Rust's testing framework allows us to write tests that verify timing constraints, priority handling, and resource management:

```rust
#[test]
fn test_priority_inheritance() {
let mut rtos = RTOS::new();
// Test setup and verification
}
```

Power management is another important consideration. We can implement different power states and transition between them based on system load and timing requirements:

```rust
pub enum PowerState {
Active,
Sleep,
DeepSleep,
Standby,
}
```

Documentation is crucial for an RTOS implementation. Rust's documentation system allows us to provide detailed explanations of API usage and safety requirements:

```rust
/// Creates a new task with the specified priority and stack size.
///
/// # Safety
///
/// The caller must ensure that the stack size is sufficient for the task's needs.
pub fn create_task(
priority: u8,
stack_size: usize,
entry_point: fn() -> (),
) -> Result<TaskId, RTOSError> {
// Implementation
}
```

When implementing an RTOS in Rust, we need to carefully consider the trade-offs between safety and performance. While Rust's zero-cost abstractions allow us to write safe code without runtime overhead, some operations necessarily require unsafe blocks. The key is to minimize the unsafe code and wrap it in safe abstractions that can be verified by the compiler.

Finally, we need to consider debugging and profiling capabilities. We can implement various debugging hooks and performance counters that can be enabled in development builds but stripped out in release builds using Rust's conditional compilation features:

```rust
#[cfg(debug_assertions)]
pub fn debug_task_state(task_id: TaskId) {
```

```
// Output debug information
}
```

An RTOS implementation in Rust provides strong safety guarantees while maintaining the performance characteristics required for real time systems. By carefully designing our APIs and leveraging Rust's type system, we can create a robust RTOS that prevents common programming errors while providing the necessary features for embedded applications.

40. Debugging Embedded Rust Applications

Debugging is a critical skill in embedded systems development, and Rust provides several powerful tools and techniques for debugging embedded applications. In this chapter, we'll explore various debugging approaches, from basic logging to advanced hardware debugging capabilities, and learn how to effectively troubleshoot issues in embedded Rust applications.

One of the fundamental debugging tools in embedded development is the serial console output. In Rust, we can implement a basic logging system using the defmt crate, which provides a lightweight formatting and logging solution specifically designed for embedded systems:

```rust
use defmt::{debug, error, info, warn};
fn process_sensor_data(reading: u16) {
info!("Processing sensor reading: {}", reading);
if reading > THRESHOLD {
warn!("Sensor reading exceeds threshold");
}
}
```

Hardware debugging is essential for embedded development, and Rust supports various debugging protocols through probe rs, a modern debugging toolkit. To set up hardware debugging, we first need to configure our project to expose the necessary debug information:

```rust
[profile.dev]
debug = true
```

```
opt-level = 0
[profile.release]
debug = true
opt-level = 3
```

The probe rs toolkit allows us to connect to various debug probes, including JTAG and SWD interfaces. We can use it programmatically in our development workflow or through command line tools. Here's an example of setting up a debug session:

```rust
use probe_rs::{Probe, Session};
fn start_debug_session() -> Result<Session, probe_rs::Error> {
let probe = Probe::list_all()
.expect("No probes found")
.pop()
.expect("No probe available");
probe.attach("nrf52840")
}
```

Breakpoints are a fundamental debugging tool, and Rust provides both software and hardware breakpoint capabilities. Software breakpoints can be implemented using the cortex_m_semihosting crate for development purposes:

```rust
use cortex_m_semihosting::hprintln;
fn critical_operation() {
#[cfg(debug_assertions)]
hprintln!("Entering critical operation").unwrap();
// Operation code here
#[cfg(debug_assertions)]
hprintln!("Exiting critical operation").unwrap();
}
```

```
```

Memory inspection is crucial for debugging embedded systems. Rust's memory safety features help prevent many common memory related bugs, but we still need tools to inspect memory contents during debugging. The probe rs toolkit provides memory inspection capabilities:

```rust
fn inspect_memory(session: &mut Session, address: u32, size: usize) {
let mut buffer = vec![0u8; size];
session.read_memory(address, &mut buffer)
.expect("Failed to read memory");
for (i, byte) in buffer.iter().enumerate() {
println!("Address 0x{:08x}: 0x{:02x}", address + i as u32, byte);
}
}
```

Register inspection is another important debugging capability. We can access CPU registers and peripheral registers during debugging sessions:

```rust
fn inspect_registers(session: &mut Session) {
let core = session.core(0).unwrap();
let registers = core.read_core_registers()
.expect("Failed to read registers");
println!("R0: {:08x}", registers.r0);
println!("PC: {:08x}", registers.pc);
}
```

Real time tracing is valuable for debugging timing related issues. Rust supports various tracing mechanisms, including ITM (Instrumentation Trace Macrocell) on ARM Cortex M devices:

```rust
use cortex_m::itm::Itm;
fn trace_execution(itm: &mut Itm) {
let stim = &mut itm.stim[0];
if stim.is_fifo_ready() {
defmt::write!(stim, "Execution trace point reached\n");
}
}
```

Exception and panic handling are critical for debugging. Rust's panic handler can be customized for embedded systems to provide useful debugging information:

```rust
#[panic_handler]
fn panic(info: &PanicInfo) -> ! {
defmt::error!("System panic: {}", defmt::Display2Format(info));
debug::exit(debug::EXIT_FAILURE);
loop {}
}
```

Conditional compilation can be used to include debug specific code without affecting release builds:

```rust
#[cfg(feature = "debugging")]
pub fn debug_output(message: &str) {
defmt::debug!("{}", message);
}
#[cfg(not(feature = "debugging"))]
pub fn debug_output(_message: &str) {}
```

Performance debugging requires special consideration in embedded systems. We can implement simple performance counters that help identify bottlenecks:

```rust
pub struct PerformanceCounter {
start_time: u32,
samples: [u32; 32],
sample_index: usize,
}
impl PerformanceCounter {
pub fn start(&mut self) {
self.start_time = DWT::get_cycle_count();
}
pub fn stop(&mut self) {
let elapsed = DWT::get_cycle_count() - self.start_time;
self.samples[self.sample_index] = elapsed;
self.sample_index = (self.sample_index + 1) % 32;
}
}
```

Remote debugging capabilities are essential for embedded systems deployed in the field. We can implement a remote debugging interface using various communication protocols:

```rust
pub struct RemoteDebugger {
connection: TcpStream,
buffer: [u8; 1024],
}
impl RemoteDebugger {
pub fn capture_state(&mut self) -> Result<(), DebugError> {
let state = system_state();
self.connection.write_all(&state.serialize())?;
```

```
Ok(())
}
}
```

Finally, it's important to implement proper error reporting and diagnostic capabilities that can help identify issues in production environments:

```rust
pub struct DiagnosticReport {
timestamp: u64,
error_code: u32,
system_state: SystemState,
call_stack: [u32; 16],
}
impl DiagnosticReport {
pub fn generate() -> Self {
Self {
timestamp: get_system_time(),
error_code: last_error_code(),
system_state: capture_system_state(),
call_stack: backtrace::capture(),
}
}
}
```

Effective debugging of embedded Rust applications requires a combination of tools, techniques, and proper instrumentation. By leveraging Rust's safety features and the available debugging tools, we can create robust debugging solutions that help identify and resolve issues efficiently while maintaining the reliability requirements of embedded systems.

41. Testing Strategies for Embedded Systems

Testing is a crucial aspect of embedded systems development that helps ensure reliability, safety, and correct functionality. In embedded Rust, we have several testing strategies available that cater to different aspects of the system, from unit testing individual components to integration testing of complete subsystems.

Unit testing in embedded Rust presents unique challenges due to hardware dependencies. One effective approach is to use mock objects and dependency injection to isolate components for testing. The embedded hal traits make this particularly convenient:

```rust
pub trait TemperatureSensor {
fn read_temperature(&mut self) -> Result<f32, SensorError>;
}
struct MockSensor {
readings: Vec<f32>
}
impl TemperatureSensor for MockSensor {
fn read_temperature(&mut self) -> Result<f32, SensorError> {
Ok(self.readings.pop().unwrap_or(25.0))
}
}
```

Testing hardware abstractions requires careful consideration of the hardware interface. We can create test harnesses that simulate hardware behavior:

```rust
pub struct TestableGpio {
state: bool,
```

```
transition_count: usize,
}
impl OutputPin for TestableGpio {
type Error = ();
fn set_high(&mut self) -> Result<(), Self::Error> {
self.state = true;
self.transition_count += 1;
Ok(())
}
}
```

Integration testing in embedded systems often involves testing communication between different subsystems. We can create test scenarios that verify correct interaction:

```rust
#[test]
fn test_sensor_communication_protocol() {
let mut mock_i2c = MockI2c::new();
let mut sensor = SensorDriver::new(mock_i2c);
mock_i2c.expect_write()
.with(eq([0x1D, 0x84]))
.returns(Ok(()));
assert!(sensor.initialize().is_ok());
}
```

Property based testing is particularly valuable for embedded systems, as it can help identify edge cases and unexpected behavior. The proptest crate can be used to generate test cases:

```rust
proptest! {
#[test]
fn test_adc_conversion(raw_value in 0u16..4096) {
```

```
let voltage = convert_adc_reading(raw_value);
assert!(voltage >= 0.0 && voltage <= 3.3);
}
}
```

Testing timing critical code requires special consideration. We can implement timing simulators for testing:

```rust
struct TimingSimulator {
current_time: u64,
events: Vec<(u64, Box<dyn Fn()>)>,
}
impl TimingSimulator {
fn schedule_event(&mut self, delay: u64, event: Box<dyn Fn()>) {
self.events.push((self.current_time + delay, event));
}
fn run(&mut self) {
while let Some((time, event)) = self.events.pop() {
self.current_time = time;
event();
}
}
}
```

Hardware in the loop (HIL) testing is essential for verifying system behavior with actual hardware. We can create test frameworks that interact with real devices:

```rust
struct HilTestFramework {
device: Device,
test_points: Vec<TestPoint>,
```

```
measurements: Vec<Measurement>,
}
impl HilTestFramework {
fn run_test_sequence(&mut self) -> TestResult {
for test_point in &self.test_points {
self.device.apply_stimulus(test_point.stimulus);
let measurement = self.device.measure_response();
self.measurements.push(measurement);
}
self.evaluate_results()
}
}
```

Continuous testing during development can be automated using test runners specifically designed for embedded systems:

```rust
use embedded_test_runner::{TestRunner, TestCase};
struct EmbeddedTestRunner {
cases: Vec<TestCase>,
results: Vec<TestResult>,
}
impl TestRunner for EmbeddedTestRunner {
fn run_tests(&mut self) -> TestSummary {
for case in &self.cases {
let result = self.execute_test(case);
self.results.push(result);
}
self.generate_summary()
}
}
```

Fault injection testing helps verify system behavior under error conditions:

```rust
struct FaultInjector {
fault_points: Vec<FaultPoint>,
active_faults: HashSet<FaultId>,
}
impl FaultInjector {
fn inject_fault(&mut self, fault_id: FaultId) {
self.active_faults.insert(fault_id);
self.trigger_fault_condition(fault_id);
}
fn clear_faults(&mut self) {
self.active_faults.clear();
self.restore_normal_operation();
}
}
```

Performance testing is crucial for real time systems. We can create benchmarks that measure execution time and resource usage:

```rust
pub struct PerformanceTest {
start_cycles: u32,
max_cycles: u32,
samples: Vec<u32>,
}
impl PerformanceTest {
fn measure_execution_time<F>(&mut self, test_fn: F)
where F: Fn() {
self.start_cycles = cycle_count();
test_fn();
let elapsed = cycle_count() - self.start_cycles;
```

self.samples.push(elapsed);
}
}
```

Coverage testing helps ensure that all code paths are exercised:

```rust
#[cfg(test)]
mod tests {
use coverage_tracker::CoverageTracker;
static COVERAGE: CoverageTracker = CoverageTracker::new();
#[test]
fn test_with_coverage() {
COVERAGE.start();
// Test code here
COVERAGE.stop();
assert!(COVERAGE.get_coverage() > 0.85);
}
}
```

Memory testing is particularly important in embedded systems with limited resources:

```rust
struct MemoryTest {
allocator: &'static mut Allocator,
peak_usage: usize,
current_usage: usize,
}
impl MemoryTest {
fn track_allocation(&mut self, size: usize) {
self.current_usage += size;
self.peak_usage = self.peak_usage.max(self.current_usage);

```
    }
}
```

Testing embedded systems requires a comprehensive approach that combines various testing strategies. By implementing these testing methodologies and maintaining good test coverage, we can build more reliable and robust embedded systems while leveraging Rust's safety guarantees.

42. Continuous Integration for Embedded Projects

Continuous Integration (CI) for embedded projects presents unique challenges that require specialized approaches and tools. Unlike traditional software development, embedded CI pipelines must account for hardware dependencies, cross compilation requirements, and platform specific testing needs.

Setting up a CI pipeline for embedded Rust projects typically begins with selecting an appropriate CI platform. Popular choices include Jenkins, GitLab CI, and GitHub Actions. Each platform offers different advantages, but the core principles remain consistent. Let's examine a typical GitHub Actions workflow for an embedded Rust project:

```yaml
name: Embedded CI Pipeline
on: [push, pull_request]
jobs:
build_and_test:
runs-on: ubuntu-latest
steps:
- uses: actions/checkout@v2
- name: Install cross compilation tools
run: |
sudo apt-get update
sudo apt-get install -y gcc-arm-none-eabi
- name: Install Rust toolchain
uses: actions-rs/toolchain@v1
with:
toolchain: nightly
target: thumbv7em-none-eabihf
```

override: true
```

The CI pipeline should include several key stages. The first is the build verification stage, which ensures that the code compiles correctly for all target platforms. This often involves cross compilation for multiple architectures:

```rust
fn verify_build_matrix() {
let targets = vec![
"thumbv6m-none-eabi",
"thumbv7m-none-eabi",
"thumbv7em-none-eabihf",
];
for target in targets {
Command::new("cargo")
.args(&["build", "—target", target])
.status()
.expect("Build failed");
}
}
```

Static analysis is another crucial component of the CI pipeline. Tools like clippy help maintain code quality and catch potential issues early:

```yaml
- name: Run clippy
run: |
cargo clippy—all-targets—all-features—-D warnings
cargo clippy—target thumbv7em-none-eabihf—-D warnings
```

Automated testing in CI requires careful consideration of hardware dependencies. For tests that require hardware access, we
```

can implement hardware simulation or use development boards connected to CI runners:

```rust
struct CiTestEnvironment {
simulated_hardware: Option<HardwareSimulator>,
physical_hardware: Option<DeviceConnection>,
}
impl CiTestEnvironment {
fn run_test_suite(&mut self) -> TestResults {
if let Some(sim) = &mut self.simulated_hardware {
self.run_simulated_tests(sim)
} else if let Some(device) = &mut self.physical_hardware {
self.run_hardware_tests(device)
} else {
self.run_unit_tests()
}
}
}
```

Documentation generation should be automated as part of the CI process. This includes both API documentation and any embedded specific documentation:

```rust
fn generate_documentation() {
Command::new("cargo")
.args(&["doc", "—no-deps", "—all-features"])
.status()
.expect("Documentation generation failed");
generate_hardware_diagrams();
update_pin_mappings();
create_deployment_guides();
}
```

```
```

Binary artifact generation and verification is essential for embedded projects. The CI pipeline should produce properly formatted binary files and verify their integrity:

```rust
fn create_release_artifacts() {
// Generate binary
Command::new("cargo")
.args(&["objcopy", "—release", "—", "-O", "binary", "firmware.bin"])
.status()
.expect("Binary generation failed");
// Verify binary size
let metadata = fs::metadata("firmware.bin").unwrap();
assert!(metadata.len() <= MAX_FIRMWARE_SIZE);
// Calculate checksums
let mut hasher = Sha256::new();
hasher.update(&fs::read("firmware.bin").unwrap());
let hash = hasher.finalize();
// Store release artifacts
fs::write("firmware.sha256", hash).unwrap();
}
```

Dependency management in CI requires special attention for embedded projects. The pipeline should verify that all dependencies are compatible with the target architecture and meet size constraints:

```rust
fn verify_dependencies() {
let metadata = cargo_metadata::MetadataCommand::new()
.exec()
.expect("Failed to get metadata");
```

```
for package in metadata.packages {
verify_package_compatibility(&package);
check_size_impact(&package);
}
}
```

Integration with hardware testing facilities can be achieved through specialized CI runners:

```rust
struct HardwareTestRunner {
device_pool: DevicePool,
test_queue: Vec<TestCase>,
results: TestResults,
}
impl HardwareTestRunner {
fn execute_test_suite(&mut self) -> TestResults {
while let Some(test) = self.test_queue.pop() {
if let Some(device) = self.device_pool.acquire_device() {
let result = self.run_test_on_device(&test, device);
self.results.record(result);
self.device_pool.release_device(device);
}
}
self.results.clone()
}
}
```

Performance benchmarking should be integrated into the CI pipeline to catch performance regressions:

```rust
fn run_performance_benchmarks() {
let mut benchmark_suite = BenchmarkSuite::new();
```

```
benchmark_suite.add_benchmark("interrupt_latency",
measure_interrupt_latency);
benchmark_suite.add_benchmark("memory_usage",
measure_memory_usage);
benchmark_suite.add_benchmark("power_consumption",
measure_power_consumption);
let results = benchmark_suite.run();
results.compare_with_baseline();
}
```

Finally, the CI pipeline should include deployment staging and release management:

```rust
fn prepare_release() {
// Version verification
verify_semantic_version();
// Changelog generation
generate_changelog();
// Release artifact preparation
package_firmware();
generate_deployment_package();
// Release verification
verify_release_package();
run_smoke_tests();
}
```

A well configured CI pipeline for embedded Rust projects helps maintain code quality, ensures reliable builds, and streamlines the release process. By automating these aspects of development, teams can focus on implementing features while maintaining confidence in their code's reliability and correctness.

Remember to regularly review and update CI configurations as project requirements evolve and new tools become available. This ensures that the CI pipeline continues to serve its purpose effectively and efficiently throughout the project's lifecycle.

43. Performance Optimization Techniques

Performance optimization is a critical aspect of embedded systems development, where resources are constrained and efficiency directly impacts the success of the final product. When optimizing embedded Rust applications, developers must consider multiple dimensions including CPU usage, memory efficiency, power consumption, and real time responsiveness.

One of the primary techniques for performance optimization in embedded Rust is the effective use of zero cost abstractions. These allow developers to write high level, maintainable code without sacrificing runtime performance. Consider the following example of a zero cost state machine implementation:

```rust
enum State {
Idle,
Processing,
Transmitting,
}
struct StateMachine<T> {
state: State,
data: T,
}
impl<T> StateMachine<T> {
#[inline(always)]
fn transition(&mut self, new_state: State) {
self.state = new_state;
}
}
```

The compiler will optimize this high level representation to be as efficient as hand written assembly, while maintaining the benefits of type safety and clear code organization.

Loop optimization is another crucial area for embedded systems. Rust's iterator abstractions can be particularly powerful here, as they often compile to optimal machine code. However, developers must be careful with iterator chains that might introduce unnecessary overhead:

```rust
fn process_sensor_data(readings: &[u16]) -> u32 {
// This will be optimized to efficient machine code
readings.iter()
.filter(|&&x| x > 100)
.map(|&x| x as u32)
.sum()
}
```

Inline assembly can be used when absolute control over CPU instructions is required, though this should be used judiciously:

```rust
use core::arch::asm;
fn fast_gpio_toggle() {
unsafe {
asm!(
"str r0, [r1]",
in("r0") (1 << 5),
in("r1") (0x40020000 as *mut u32),
);
}
}
```

Memory access patterns play a crucial role in performance optimization. Proper alignment and cache friendly data structures can significantly impact execution speed:

```rust
#[repr(align(4))]
struct AlignedBuffer {
data: [u8; 1024],
}
fn process_aligned_data(buffer: &AlignedBuffer) {
for chunk in buffer.data.chunks(4) {
// Process 4 byte aligned chunks
}
}
```

When working with interrupts, careful optimization of interrupt handlers is essential for maintaining system responsiveness:

```rust
#[interrupt]
fn TIMER0() {
static mut COUNTER: u32 = 0;
// Minimize time spent in interrupt handler
*COUNTER = COUNTER.wrapping_add(1);
// Clear interrupt flag quickly
unsafe {
(*TIMER0::ptr()).clear_interrupt();
}
}
```

Power optimization often involves careful management of sleep states and peripheral usage. Rust's type system can help enforce power efficient patterns:

```rust
```

```rust
struct PowerManager<T> {
peripheral: T,
current_state: PowerState,
}
impl<T: Peripheral> PowerManager<T> {
fn enter_low_power_mode(&mut self) {
self.peripheral.disable();
self.current_state = PowerState::LowPower;
// Configure system clock
unsafe {
configure_low_power_clock();
}
}
}
```

Binary size optimization is crucial for embedded systems with limited flash memory. The use of appropriate compiler flags and careful attention to dependencies can help:

```toml
[profile.release]
opt-level = "z"
lto = true
codegen-units = 1
panic = "abort"
```

Runtime performance can be improved through strategic use of static dispatch over dynamic dispatch when possible:

```rust
trait SensorInterface {
fn read_value(&self) -> u16;
}
// Using static dispatch
```

```
fn process_reading<T: SensorInterface>(sensor: &T) -> u16 {
sensor.read_value()
}
// Instead of dynamic dispatch
fn process_reading_dynamic(sensor: &dyn SensorInterface) ->
u16 {
sensor.read_value()
}
```

SIMD operations can be utilized when available on the target architecture:

```rust
#[cfg(target_arch = "arm")]
use core::arch::arm::*;
fn optimize_data_processing(data: &mut [u32]) {
#[cfg(target_arch = "arm")]
unsafe {
if is_arm_feature_detected!("neon") {
// Use NEON SIMD instructions
process_with_neon(data);
}
}
}
```

Memory allocation patterns should be optimized to minimize fragmentation and allocation overhead:

```rust
use alloc::boxed::Box;
use alloc::vec::Vec;
struct PoolAllocator<T> {
free_list: Vec<Box<T>>,
capacity: usize,
```

```
}
impl<T> PoolAllocator<T> {
fn allocate(&mut self) -> Option<Box<T>> {
self.free_list.pop()
}
fn deallocate(&mut self, item: Box<T>) {
if self.free_list.len() < self.capacity {
self.free_list.push(item);
}
}
}
```

Performance profiling should be integrated into the development process to identify bottlenecks and verify optimizations:

```rust
fn profile_critical_section<F>(name: &str, f: F)
where
F: FnOnce(),
{
let start = cycle_count();
f();
let end = cycle_count();
log::info!("{} took {} cycles", name, end - start);
}
```

Remember that premature optimization can lead to more complex, harder to maintain code without significant benefits. Always profile first to identify where optimization efforts will have the most impact. The best optimization strategy often involves finding the right balance between code clarity, maintainability, and performance requirements specific to your embedded application.

Through careful application of these optimization techniques, embedded Rust applications can achieve excellent performance while maintaining the safety and reliability guarantees that make Rust an excellent choice for embedded systems development.

44. Memory Optimization Strategies

Chapter 44 focuses on memory optimization strategies for embedded Rust systems, where efficient memory usage is paramount due to the constrained resources typical of embedded devices.

Memory optimization in embedded Rust begins with understanding the different memory regions available in a typical embedded system. Program code and constant data reside in flash memory, while variables and runtime data occupy RAM. Efficient use of these regions requires careful consideration of data structures and their placement.

Static allocation is preferred in embedded systems whenever possible, as it provides predictable memory usage and avoids fragmentation. Rust's const generics feature is particularly useful for creating fixed size data structures:

```rust
struct CircularBuffer<const N: usize> {
data: [u8; N],
read_index: usize,
write_index: usize,
}
impl<const N: usize> CircularBuffer<N> {
const fn new() -> Self{
Self{
data: [0; N],
read_index: 0,
write_index: 0,
}
}
}
```

When working with strings in embedded systems, using static strings can significantly reduce RAM usage. The compile time string handling capabilities of Rust make this particularly effective:

```rust
use core::fmt::Write;
static ERROR_MESSAGES: &[&str] = &[
"Sensor initialization failed",
"Communication timeout",
"Buffer overflow",
];
fn get_error_message(index: usize) -> &'static str {
ERROR_MESSAGES.get(index).unwrap_or(&"Unknown
error")
}
```

Memory pooling is another crucial strategy for managing dynamic allocation needs without the overhead and unpredictability of a heap allocator. A simple memory pool implementation might look like this:

```rust
struct MemoryPool<T, const N: usize> {
storage: [Option<T>; N],
free_list: [bool; N],
}
impl<T, const N: usize> MemoryPool<T, N> {
fn allocate(&mut self) -> Option<&mut T> {
for (index, is_free) in self.free_list.iter_mut().enumerate() {
if *is_free {
*is_free = false;
return self.storage[index].as_mut();
}
}
```

```
None
}
}
```

Bit fields can be used to pack multiple values into a single byte or word, reducing memory usage for small values. Rust's bitfield crates provide safe abstractions for this:

```rust
use bitfield::bitfield;
bitfield! {
struct SensorStatus(u8);
impl Debug;
pub active, set_active: 0;
pub error, set_error: 1;
pub calibrated, set_calibrated: 2;
pub temperature, set_temperature: 3, 7;
}
```

When working with collections, choosing the right data structure can significantly impact memory usage. For example, using a fixed capacity Vec can prevent unexpected memory growth:

```rust
use heapless::Vec;
struct SensorReadings {
data: Vec<u16, 64>, // Maximum capacity of 64 elements
}
impl SensorReadings {
fn add_reading(&mut self, value: u16) -> Result<(), ()> {
self.data.push(value)
}
}
```

Memory mapped peripherals should be accessed efficiently to minimize RAM usage for peripheral control:

```rust
use core::ptr::{read_volatile, write_volatile};
struct GPIO {
base_address: *mut u32,
}
impl GPIO {
fn set_pin(&mut self, pin: u8, state: bool) {
let offset = if state { 0x18 } else { 0x1C };
unsafe {
write_volatile(
self.base_address.add(offset as usize),
1 << pin
);
}
}
}
```

Stack usage optimization is critical in embedded systems. Using const functions can help move computations to compile time:

```rust
const fn calculate_lookup_table() -> [u16; 256] {
let mut table = [0u16; 256];
let mut i = 0;
while i < 256 {
table[i] = (i as u16).wrapping_mul(123);
i += 1;
}
table
}
```

```rust
static LOOKUP_TABLE: [u16; 256] = calculate_lookup_table();
```

Memory fragmentation can be minimized by using appropriate alignment and padding in data structures:

```rust
#[repr(C)]
#[derive(Copy, Clone)]
struct AlignedPacket {
header: u32,
#[cfg(target_arch = "arm")]
_padding: [u8; 2],
payload: [u8; 64],
checksum: u16,
}
```

For systems requiring dynamic memory allocation, implementing a custom allocator can provide better control over memory usage:

```rust
use core::alloc::{GlobalAlloc, Layout};
struct BumpAllocator {
heap_start: usize,
heap_end: usize,
next: usize,
}
unsafe impl GlobalAlloc for BumpAllocator {
unsafe fn alloc(&self, layout: Layout) -> *mut u8 {
let alloc_start = align_up(self.next, layout.align());
let alloc_end = alloc_start.saturating_add(layout.size());
if alloc_end <= self.heap_end {
self.next = alloc_end;
```

```
alloc_start as *mut u8
} else {
core::ptr::null_mut()
}
}
unsafe fn dealloc(&self, _ptr: *mut u8, _layout: Layout) {
// This allocator never deallocates
}
}
```

Using const generics for compile time array sizing can help prevent runtime memory allocation:

```rust
struct RingBuffer<T, const N: usize> {
buffer: [T; N],
read_ptr: usize,
write_ptr: usize,
}
impl<T: Default + Copy, const N: usize> RingBuffer<T, N> {
const fn new() -> Self {
Self {
buffer: [T::default(); N],
read_ptr: 0,
write_ptr: 0,
}
}
}
```

Memory optimization is an ongoing process that requires careful attention to both the initial design and continuous monitoring of memory usage patterns. Regular profiling and testing under various conditions help ensure that memory optimizations are effective and don't introduce new problems. The key is finding the right balance between memory efficiency and code maintainability while maintaining Rust's safety guarantees.

45. Error Handling in Embedded Systems

Chapter 45 focuses on error handling strategies for embedded systems, a critical aspect of building reliable and robust embedded applications.

Error handling in embedded systems presents unique challenges due to resource constraints and the need for predictable behavior. Unlike desktop applications, embedded systems often cannot simply crash and restart when encountering errors. They must gracefully handle failures while maintaining system stability and safety.

Rust's error handling mechanisms provide excellent tools for embedded development. The Result type is particularly valuable as it forces explicit error handling without runtime overhead. Here's a typical pattern for handling hardware initialization:

```rust
pub enum InitError {
SensorNotFound,
CalibrationFailed,
InvalidConfiguration,
TimerSetupFailed,
}
fn initialize_hardware() -> Result<(), InitError> {
setup_sensors().map_err(|_| InitError::SensorNotFound)?;
calibrate_system().map_err(|_| InitError::CalibrationFailed)?;
configure_peripherals().map_err(|_|
InitError::InvalidConfiguration)?;
setup_timer().map_err(|_| InitError::TimerSetupFailed)?;
Ok(())
}
```

For resource constrained systems, compact error types are essential. Instead of using string based errors, numeric error codes or small enums can significantly reduce memory usage:

```rust
#[derive(Debug, Copy, Clone)]
#[repr(u8)]
pub enum SystemError {
None = 0,
SensorFailure = 1,
CommunicationTimeout = 2,
BufferOverflow = 3,
InvalidState = 4,
}
impl SystemError {
fn to_led_pattern(self) -> u8 {
match self {
SystemError::None => 0b0000_0000,
SystemError::SensorFailure => 0b0000_0001,
SystemError::CommunicationTimeout => 0b0000_0010,
SystemError::BufferOverflow => 0b0000_0100,
SystemError::InvalidState => 0b0000_1000,
}
}
}
```

Error recovery strategies are crucial in embedded systems. A tiered approach to error handling can help manage different severity levels:

```rust
enum ErrorSeverity {
Warning,
Recoverable,
```

```
Critical,
}
struct ErrorHandler {
current_state: SystemState,
error_count: u32,
last_error: Option<SystemError>,
}
impl ErrorHandler {
fn handle_error(&mut self, error: SystemError, severity: ErrorSeverity) {
match severity {
ErrorSeverity::Warning => {
self.log_warning(error);
self.attempt_recovery();
}
ErrorSeverity::Recoverable => {
self.log_error(error);
self.increment_error_count();
self.reset_subsystem();
}
ErrorSeverity::Critical => {
self.log_critical(error);
self.emergency_shutdown();
}
}
}
}
```

For communication protocols, error handling often needs to account for timeouts and retry mechanisms:

```rust
struct CommController {
```

```
retries: u8,
timeout_ms: u32,
}
impl CommController {
fn send_with_retry<T>(&mut self, data: &[u8]) -> Result<T, CommError> {
let mut attempts = 0;
while attempts < self.retries {
match self.send_data(data) {
Ok(response) => return Ok(response),
Err(CommError::Timeout) => {
attempts += 1;
continue;
}
Err(e) => return Err(e),
}
}
Err(CommError::MaxRetriesExceeded)
}
}
```

Non recoverable errors in embedded systems often require careful handling to ensure system safety:

```rust
#[inline(never)]
fn handle_panic(info: &PanicInfo) -> ! {
// Disable interrupts to prevent further issues
critical_section::with(|_| {
// Log panic information to non volatile storage
if let Some(location) = info.location() {
log_to_flash(location.file(), location.line());
}
```

```
// Ensure all peripherals are in a safe state
unsafe {
disable_all_peripherals();
}
// Trigger watchdog reset or enter infinite loop
loop {
// Blink error LED or similar indicator
indicate_fatal_error();
}
})
}
```

Error logging in embedded systems requires careful consideration of storage limitations:

```rust
struct CircularErrorLog<const N: usize> {
entries: [Option<ErrorEntry>; N],
write_index: usize,
}
impl<const N: usize> CircularErrorLog<N> {
fn log_error(&mut self, error: SystemError, timestamp: u32) {
let entry = ErrorEntry {
error,
timestamp,
context: get_system_context(),
};
self.entries[self.write_index] = Some(entry);
self.write_index = (self.write_index + 1) % N;
}
}
```

For systems with multiple subsystems, hierarchical error handling can help manage complexity:

```rust
struct SubsystemManager {
sensors: SensorSubsystem,
communication: CommSubsystem,
control: ControlSubsystem,
}
impl SubsystemManager {
fn handle_subsystem_error(&mut self, error: SubsystemError) -> Result<(), SystemError> {
match error {
SubsystemError::Sensor(e) => self.handle_sensor_error(e),
SubsystemError::Communication(e) => self.handle_comm_error(e),
SubsystemError::Control(e) => self.handle_control_error(e),
}
}
}
```

Error handling in interrupt contexts requires special consideration:

```rust
static ERROR_FLAG: AtomicBool = AtomicBool::new(false);
static ERROR_CODE: AtomicU8 = AtomicU8::new(0);
#[interrupt]
fn TIMER0() {
if let Err(e) = handle_timer_interrupt() {
// Store error information atomically
ERROR_FLAG.store(true, Ordering::Relaxed);
ERROR_CODE.store(e as u8, Ordering::Relaxed);
}
```

```
}
fn main_loop() {
if ERROR_FLAG.load(Ordering::Relaxed) {
let error_code = ERROR_CODE.load(Ordering::Relaxed);
handle_interrupt_error(error_code);
ERROR_FLAG.store(false, Ordering::Relaxed);
}
}
```

Proper error handling is fundamental to building reliable embedded systems. By leveraging Rust's type system and zero cost abstractions, we can implement robust error handling strategies that maintain system safety without compromising performance or resource usage. The key is to design error handling mechanisms that are appropriate for the specific constraints and requirements of the embedded system while ensuring that no error condition can lead to undefined behavior or system instability.

46. Logging and Monitoring

Chapter 46 focuses on implementing effective logging and monitoring systems for embedded devices, essential components for debugging, maintenance, and system health tracking.

Logging in embedded systems presents unique challenges due to limited resources and storage constraints. Unlike traditional computing environments, embedded systems often lack permanent storage or network connectivity for continuous log transmission. This requires careful consideration of logging strategies and efficient use of available resources.

A basic logging framework for embedded systems might start with a circular buffer implementation that efficiently manages limited memory:

```rust
struct CircularLogger {
buffer: &'static mut [u8],
write_position: usize,
wrapped: bool,
}
impl CircularLogger {
pub fn log(&mut self, message: &[u8]) {
for byte in message {
self.buffer[self.write_position] = *byte;
self.write_position = (self.write_position + 1) % self.buffer.len();
if self.write_position == 0 {
self.wrapped = true;
}
}
}
```

```
}
```

Different severity levels help prioritize log messages and manage storage space effectively. A common approach is to define multiple log levels:

```rust
#[derive(Copy, Clone)]
pub enum LogLevel {
Error = 1,
Warning = 2,
Info = 3,
Debug = 4,
}
struct LogEntry {
timestamp: u32,
level: LogLevel,
module: u8,
message: [u8; 32],
}
```

Real time monitoring requires efficient data collection and processing. One approach is to use a ring buffer for collecting metrics:

```rust
struct MetricsCollector {
temperature_readings: [i16; 64],
voltage_readings: [u16; 64],
current_index: usize,
sample_count: u32,
}
impl MetricsCollector {
```

```
pub fn record_metrics(&mut self, temperature: i16, voltage: u16) {
self.temperature_readings[self.current_index] = temperature;
self.voltage_readings[self.current_index] = voltage;
self.current_index = (self.current_index + 1) % 64;
self.sample_count = self.sample_count.saturating_add(1);
}
}
```

For systems with network connectivity, implementing a remote logging capability can be valuable:

```rust
struct NetworkLogger {
buffer: [LogEntry; 32],
network_interface: NetworkInterface,
transmission_pending: bool,
}
impl NetworkLogger {
pub fn transmit_logs(&mut self) -> Result<(), NetworkError> {
if self.transmission_pending {
self.network_interface.send_buffer(&self.buffer)?;
self.transmission_pending = false;
}
Ok(())
}
}
```

System health monitoring is crucial for maintaining reliable operation. A health monitor might track various system parameters:

```rust
struct SystemHealth {
```

```rust
uptime: u32,
memory_usage: u32,
cpu_load: u8,
temperature: i16,
voltage: u16,
error_count: u32,
}
impl SystemHealth {
pub fn update(&mut self) {
self.uptime = get_system_ticks();
self.memory_usage = measure_heap_usage();
self.cpu_load = calculate_cpu_load();
self.temperature = read_temperature();
self.voltage = read_system_voltage();
}
}
```

For systems with limited storage, compression techniques can help maximize log storage capacity:

```rust
struct CompressedLogger {
dictionary: [&'static str; 64],
compressed_buffer: [u8; 1024],
write_index: usize,
}
impl CompressedLogger {
pub fn log_compressed(&mut self, message: &str) {
if let Some(dictionary_index) = self.find_in_dictionary(message) {
self.compressed_buffer[self.write_index] = dictionary_index as u8;
self.write_index += 1;
```

```
} else {
self.store_full_message(message);
}
}
}
```

Performance monitoring requires careful tracking of timing and resource usage:

```rust
struct PerformanceMonitor {
execution_times: [u32; 16],
function_ids: [u8; 16],
current_index: usize,
}
impl PerformanceMonitor {
pub fn record_execution_time(&mut self, function_id: u8, duration: u32) {
self.execution_times[self.current_index] = duration;
self.function_ids[self.current_index] = function_id;
self.current_index = (self.current_index + 1) % 16;
}
}
```

For systems requiring persistent logging, flash memory can be utilized efficiently:

```rust
struct FlashLogger {
current_sector: u8,
write_position: u32,
sectors_used: u32,
}
impl FlashLogger {
```

```
pub fn write_to_flash(&mut self, data: &[u8]) -> Result<(),
FlashError> {
if self.write_position + data.len() as u32 > SECTOR_SIZE {
self.switch_sector()?;
}
self.write_data(data)?;
self.write_position += data.len() as u32;
Ok(())
}
}
```

Monitoring system resources often requires tracking multiple metrics simultaneously:

```rust
struct ResourceMonitor {
stack_usage: StackMonitor,
heap_usage: HeapMonitor,
cpu_usage: CpuMonitor,
}
impl ResourceMonitor {
pub fn collect_metrics(&mut self) -> SystemMetrics {
SystemMetrics {
stack_remaining: self.stack_usage.get_remaining(),
heap_allocated: self.heap_usage.get_allocated(),
cpu_percentage: self.cpu_usage.get_percentage(),
}
}
}
```

Effective logging and monitoring systems are essential for maintaining and debugging embedded systems. By carefully considering resource constraints and implementing efficient data collection and storage strategies, we can create robust monitoring solutions that provide valuable insights into system operation without overwhelming limited system resources. The key is to balance the need for detailed system information with the practical limitations of embedded hardware.

47. Sensor Integration

Sensor integration represents a fundamental aspect of embedded systems development, bridging the physical world with digital processing capabilities. This chapter explores implementing robust sensor systems in Rust, focusing on accurate data acquisition, efficient processing, and reliable error handling across various sensor types and communication protocols.

• • • •

SENSOR ABSTRACTION forms the foundation of effective integration. We'll examine creating flexible sensor interfaces using Rust traits, allowing us to implement consistent APIs across different sensor types while maintaining type safety. This abstraction layer enables us to handle various sensors - from simple analog devices to complex digital sensors - through a unified interface while preserving their unique characteristics and capabilities.

• • • •

SIGNAL CONDITIONING and calibration play crucial roles in obtaining accurate sensor readings. We'll implement signal processing chains that handle analog-to-digital conversion, filtering, and calibration. Rust's type system helps prevent common errors in unit conversions and calculations while maintaining computational efficiency. Our implementation includes handling sensor offset compensation, gain adjustment, and temperature compensation where necessary.

• • • •

ERROR DETECTION AND handling become particularly important when working with sensors. We'll explore implementing comprehensive error checking that covers communication failures, out-of-range values, and sensor malfunction detection. This includes implementing proper timeout handling, sensor health monitoring, and recovery procedures. Rust's Result type provides a natural way to handle these error conditions while ensuring no error cases are overlooked.

• • • •

MULTIPLE SENSOR FUSION represents an advanced technique for improving measurement accuracy and reliability. We'll implement sensor fusion algorithms that combine data from complementary sensors, including Kalman filtering and complementary filters. The implementation includes proper handling of different sampling rates, sensor latencies, and measurement uncertainties. Rust's strong typing helps prevent common errors in matrix operations and statistical calculations.

• • • •

POWER MANAGEMENT FOR sensor systems requires careful consideration. We'll explore implementing power-efficient sampling strategies, including duty cycling, adaptive sampling rates, and sleep mode management. This includes proper handling of sensor warm-up times, power state transitions, and maintaining measurement accuracy while minimizing power consumption. Rust's zero-cost abstractions ensure our power management code remains efficient.

• • • •

COMMUNICATION PROTOCOL handling forms a critical part of sensor integration. We'll implement robust interfaces for common sensor protocols including I2C, SPI, and analog sampling. This includes proper timing management, protocol error handling, and efficient data transfer. Our implementation covers handling different sensor communication speeds, bus sharing, and protocol-specific requirements while maintaining system reliability.

• • • •

DATA BUFFERING AND processing often require careful management of system resources. We'll implement efficient buffer management strategies for sensor data, including circular buffers and double buffering techniques. Rust's ownership model helps prevent common buffer overflow errors while ensuring efficient memory usage. The implementation includes handling different data rates and ensuring no data loss during processing.

• • • •

REAL-TIME CONSTRAINTS frequently apply to sensor sampling and processing. We'll explore implementing deterministic sampling schedules, including handling multiple sensors with different timing requirements. This includes implementing proper interrupt handling for sensor data acquisition, maintaining sampling accuracy, and ensuring consistent processing latency. Rust's predictable performance characteristics help maintain timing requirements.

• • • •

ENVIRONMENTAL CONSIDERATIONS affect sensor operation significantly. We'll implement compensation mechanisms for environmental factors such as temperature, humidity, and electromagnetic interference. This includes implementing proper filtering techniques, environmental monitoring, and adaptive calibration procedures. Our implementation covers handling sensor cross-sensitivity and maintaining measurement accuracy across varying conditions.

• • • •

TESTING SENSOR IMPLEMENTATIONS requires specialized approaches. We'll develop comprehensive testing strategies that include sensor simulation, calibration verification, and long-term stability testing. This includes creating test fixtures for sensor characterization, implementing automated testing procedures, and ensuring proper test coverage for various operating conditions.

• • • •

DATA VALIDATION AND quality assurance play crucial roles in sensor systems. We'll implement data validation mechanisms that detect anomalous readings, sensor drift, and measurement instability. This includes implementing statistical analysis tools, trend monitoring, and data quality metrics. Rust's type system helps ensure that validation criteria are properly enforced and maintained.

• • • •

SENSOR MAINTENANCE and diagnostics require careful consideration in long-term deployments. We'll explore implementing diagnostic capabilities that monitor sensor health, detect degradation, and facilitate maintenance procedures. This includes implementing sensor self-test routines, wear monitoring, and maintenance scheduling based on sensor performance metrics.

• • • •

BY THE END OF THIS chapter, readers will understand how to implement comprehensive sensor integration in their Rust-based embedded systems. We've seen how Rust's safety features and performance characteristics make it particularly well-suited for implementing reliable sensor systems. The combination of accurate measurement capabilities with Rust's strong guarantees creates a robust foundation for developing sophisticated sensor applications.

• • • •

THIS EXPLORATION OF sensor integration demonstrates that Rust provides an excellent foundation for implementing sensor systems in embedded applications. Whether creating measurement systems, monitoring applications, or control systems, Rust's safety guarantees and performance characteristics make it an ideal choice for sensor integration, ensuring reliable and accurate operation while preventing common programming errors.

48. Display Interfaces

Display interfaces form a crucial component of many embedded systems, providing visual feedback and user interaction capabilities. This chapter explores implementing robust display systems in Rust, focusing on efficient graphics handling, memory management, and performance optimization while maintaining code safety and reliability.

• • • •

DISPLAY ABSTRACTION serves as our starting point, implementing traits that provide a consistent interface across different display technologies. We'll create abstractions that handle everything from simple seven-segment displays to complex graphic LCDs and OLED panels. Rust's trait system allows us to create flexible, reusable display drivers while maintaining type safety and ensuring efficient runtime performance.

• • • •

BUFFER MANAGEMENT PLAYS a critical role in display systems. We'll examine implementing both single and double-buffering strategies, managing frame buffers efficiently while preventing tearing and visual artifacts. Rust's ownership model helps prevent common issues like buffer overruns and race conditions when updating display contents. We'll explore techniques for partial updates and dirty region tracking to optimize refresh performance.

• • • •

GRAPHICS PRIMITIVES form the foundation of any display system. We'll implement efficient routines for basic shapes, lines, circles, and text rendering. This includes optimized algorithms for fill operations, anti-aliasing, and clipping. Rust's zero-cost abstractions allow us to create high-level drawing interfaces without sacrificing performance, while the type system helps prevent common rendering errors like out-of-bounds operations.

• • • •

FONT HANDLING REQUIRES careful memory management and efficient rendering. We'll explore implementing both bitmap and vector font systems, including proper character encoding support and font scaling. Our implementation includes techniques for font caching, glyph rendering, and proper text alignment. We'll examine handling different font formats while maintaining memory efficiency on resource-constrained systems.

• • • •

COLOR MANAGEMENT BECOMES crucial when working with color displays. We'll implement color space conversions, dithering algorithms, and proper color depth handling. This includes managing different color formats, implementing gamma correction, and handling color palettes efficiently. Rust's type system helps prevent common errors in color calculations and format conversions.

• • • •

DISPLAY PROTOCOL IMPLEMENTATION requires careful attention to timing and communication efficiency. We'll explore implementing common display protocols like SPI, parallel interfaces, and MIPI DSI. This includes proper timing management, DMA transfers where applicable, and efficient command sequencing. Our implementation covers handling different display refresh rates and synchronization requirements.

• • • •

MEMORY OPTIMIZATION becomes critical when working with limited resources. We'll examine techniques for reducing memory usage through compressed framebuffers, sprite management, and efficient update strategies. This includes implementing proper memory allocation strategies and managing display memory hierarchies effectively. Rust's compile-time guarantees help ensure our optimizations don't introduce memory-related bugs.

• • • •

USER INTERFACE ELEMENTS require both efficient rendering and proper state management. We'll implement common UI widgets like buttons, progress bars, and scrolling lists. This includes handling touch input where applicable, managing widget state, and implementing proper update mechanisms. Rust's strong typing helps maintain UI consistency and prevent common state management errors.

• • • •

ANIMATION SUPPORT ADDS complexity to display systems. We'll explore implementing efficient animation frameworks, including sprite animation, transitions, and scrolling effects. This includes proper timing management, frame interpolation, and efficient resource usage. Our implementation covers handling multiple simultaneous animations while maintaining system responsiveness.

• • • •

ERROR HANDLING IN DISPLAY systems requires careful consideration. We'll implement robust error detection and recovery mechanisms for display hardware failures, communication errors, and resource exhaustion. This includes implementing proper initialization sequences, handling display reconnection, and managing failure modes gracefully. Rust's error handling patterns help create reliable recovery procedures.

••••

PERFORMANCE OPTIMIZATION becomes crucial for smooth display operation. We'll examine techniques for optimizing refresh rates, reducing CPU usage, and managing power consumption. This includes implementing hardware acceleration where available, optimizing drawing algorithms, and managing display updates efficiently. Rust's zero-cost abstractions ensure our optimizations maintain safety while improving performance.

••••

TESTING DISPLAY IMPLEMENTATIONS presents unique challenges. We'll develop testing strategies that include visual verification, performance measurement, and automated testing of drawing operations. This includes creating test frameworks for display drivers, implementing visual regression testing, and ensuring proper coverage of display functionality.

••••

BY THE END OF THIS chapter, readers will understand how to implement comprehensive display systems in their Rust-based embedded applications. We've seen how Rust's safety features and performance characteristics make it particularly well-suited for implementing reliable display interfaces. The combination of efficient graphics handling with Rust's strong guarantees creates a robust foundation for developing sophisticated display applications.

••••

THIS EXPLORATION OF display interfaces demonstrates that Rust provides an excellent foundation for implementing visual systems in embedded applications. Whether creating user interfaces, information displays, or graphic applications, Rust's safety guarantees and performance characteristics make it an ideal choice for display development, ensuring reliable and efficient operation while preventing common programming errors.

49. Audio Processing

Audio processing is a critical aspect of many embedded systems, from simple sound output devices to complex digital signal processing applications. In embedded Rust, working with audio requires careful consideration of real time constraints, buffer management, and efficient processing algorithms. This chapter explores the fundamentals of audio processing in embedded systems using Rust, covering both basic concepts and practical implementations.

At its core, digital audio processing involves working with discrete samples of sound waves. These samples are typically represented as numerical values that correspond to the amplitude of the sound wave at specific points in time. In embedded systems, we often work with different sample formats, including 8 bit, 16 bit, or 24 bit PCM (Pulse Code Modulation) data. Rust's strong type system helps us handle these different formats safely and efficiently.

Let's begin with the basics of audio input and output. Most embedded systems use either analog to digital converters (ADCs) for audio input or digital to analog converters (DACs) for audio output. In Rust, we can create type safe abstractions for these hardware interfaces. Here's how we might implement a basic audio interface:

When working with audio in embedded systems, buffer management is crucial. We need to ensure that we can process audio data fast enough to maintain real time performance while preventing buffer underruns or overruns. Rust's ownership system helps us manage audio buffers safely, preventing common issues like buffer overflow or data races in interrupt handlers.

One of the most common audio processing tasks is filtering. Digital filters can be implemented efficiently in Rust using fixed point arithmetic for resource constrained systems. For example, a simple moving average filter can reduce noise in audio signals. More complex filters like FIR (Finite Impulse Response) or IIR (Infinite Impulse Response) filters can be implemented with careful attention to numerical stability and processing efficiency.

Audio compression is another important aspect of embedded audio processing. While complex codecs like MP3 or AAC might be too resource intensive for many embedded systems, simple compression techniques can be implemented effectively. Rust's zero cost abstractions allow us to write high level code that compiles down to efficient machine instructions, making it possible to implement real time audio compression without sacrificing performance.

For systems requiring multiple audio channels, Rust's type system can help ensure correct handling of interleaved audio data. We can create strong types that represent multi channel audio formats, making it impossible to accidentally mix up channel ordering or sample alignment. This is particularly important in applications like surround sound processing or audio mixing.

Real time audio processing requires careful attention to timing constraints. In embedded systems, we often need to process audio samples within strict deadlines to maintain continuous playback or recording. Rust's predictable performance characteristics and lack of garbage collection make it well suited for these requirements. We can use hardware timers and interrupts to ensure precise timing of audio processing operations.

When implementing audio effects like reverb, delay, or equalization, we need to carefully manage memory usage and processing overhead. Rust's compile time memory management helps us allocate buffers and processing structures efficiently. For example, implementing a delay effect requires a circular buffer to store previous samples. Rust's safe abstractions allow us to implement this efficiently while preventing buffer overruns.

Digital signal processing algorithms are a fundamental part of audio processing. Fast Fourier Transforms (FFT), for instance, are commonly used for frequency analysis and spectral processing. While these algorithms can be complex, Rust's type system helps us implement them correctly and safely. We can create type safe interfaces for complex number operations and ensure proper handling of array bounds.

Error handling in audio processing requires special consideration. Unlike other types of data processing, audio glitches or discontinuities can be immediately noticeable to users. Rust's Result type helps us handle error conditions gracefully, allowing us to implement fallback behaviors or graceful degradation when problems occur.

Integration with audio codecs and hardware peripherals often requires careful management of control interfaces and configuration registers. Rust's embedded HAL traits provide a standardized way to interact with these devices, making it easier to write portable audio processing code that works across different hardware platforms.

For systems that need to process audio streams over networks or other communication interfaces, Rust's strong networking support comes in handy. We can implement efficient streaming protocols while maintaining type safety and memory safety. This is particularly important in applications like networked audio distribution or voice over IP.

Testing audio processing code presents unique challenges. We need to verify both functional correctness and real time performance. Rust's testing framework allows us to write unit tests for processing algorithms, while integration tests can verify system level behavior. We can also use Rust's benchmarking features to ensure processing performance meets our requirements.

Optimization is often critical in audio processing applications. Rust provides several tools for optimizing audio code, including

SIMD instructions for parallel processing of audio samples, careful memory alignment for efficient access patterns, and compile time optimization of mathematical operations. The compiler's zero cost abstractions ensure that high level code can be optimized to highly efficient machine code.

Finally, debugging audio processing code requires specialized tools and techniques. We can use Rust's logging and tracing facilities to monitor processing operations, while debug builds can include additional safety checks without affecting release performance. Many embedded debugging tools support capturing and analyzing audio data streams, making it easier to diagnose problems in real world applications.

Audio processing in embedded systems continues to evolve, with new applications requiring increasingly sophisticated processing capabilities. Rust's combination of safety, performance, and expressiveness makes it an excellent choice for implementing audio processing systems, from simple playback devices to complex real time processing applications.

50. USB Communication

USB Communication is a fundamental aspect of modern embedded systems, providing a versatile interface for connecting devices to computers and other peripherals. In embedded Rust, implementing USB functionality requires understanding both the protocol specifics and how to leverage Rust's safety features for reliable communication. This chapter explores USB implementation in embedded systems using Rust, from basic device enumeration to complex data transfer protocols.

The Universal Serial Bus (USB) protocol provides a standardized way to connect devices, supporting various transfer types and speeds. When implementing USB in embedded Rust, we start with the device descriptor hierarchy, which defines how the device presents itself to the host. Rust's type system helps ensure that these descriptors are correctly structured and valid according to the USB specification.

One of the key advantages of using Rust for USB implementation is the ability to create safe abstractions around the complex state machines involved in USB communication. A USB device must handle various states including attachment, enumeration, configuration, and data transfer. We can model these states using Rust's enum types and ensure that invalid state transitions are caught at compile time.

Device enumeration is the first step in USB communication, where the device identifies itself to the host. In Rust, we can create type safe representations of USB descriptors:

The implementation of USB endpoints requires careful management of data buffers and transfer states. Rust's ownership system helps prevent common issues like buffer overruns or concurrent access to endpoint buffers. We can use static buffers with proper alignment requirements, ensuring efficient data transfer while maintaining memory safety.

USB supports different transfer types including control, bulk, interrupt, and isochronous transfers. Each type has its own characteristics and requirements. Control transfers are used for device configuration and status requests, bulk transfers for large data movements, interrupt transfers for periodic small data packets, and isochronous transfers for real time data streams. Rust allows us to create specific abstractions for each transfer type while sharing common infrastructure.

Error handling is crucial in USB communication, as various conditions can disrupt the connection or data transfer. Rust's Result type provides a natural way to handle USB errors, allowing us to implement robust recovery mechanisms. We can define specific error types for different USB related issues, making it clear what went wrong and how to handle it.

When implementing USB device classes like HID (Human Interface Device), CDC (Communication Device Class), or Mass Storage, Rust's trait system helps create clean interfaces that enforce protocol requirements. We can define traits for different device classes and implement them for specific hardware, ensuring that all required functionality is provided.

Buffer management is a critical aspect of USB communication. We need to handle both IN and OUT endpoints, managing data transfer in both directions. Rust's zero copy abstractions allow us to efficiently handle data buffers while preventing memory corruption:

Real time constraints often apply to USB communication, particularly for interrupt and isochronous transfers. Rust's predictable performance characteristics help ensure that we can meet these timing requirements. We can use hardware features like DMA (Direct Memory Access) efficiently while maintaining safety guarantees.

USB debugging presents unique challenges, as problems can occur at various protocol layers. Rust's strong typing helps catch many issues at compile time, while runtime checks can help identify protocol violations. We can implement debugging features that log USB events and state transitions without affecting release performance.

Power management is an important consideration in USB devices. Many devices need to support different power states and respond to USB suspend and resume events. Rust helps us manage these power state transitions safely, ensuring that all required cleanup operations are performed when entering low power states.

Testing USB implementations requires both unit testing of protocol handling code and integration testing with actual hardware. Rust's testing framework allows us to verify protocol compliance in isolation, while integration tests can validate behavior with real USB hosts:

When implementing custom USB protocols, Rust's type system helps ensure protocol consistency. We can create strong types for protocol messages and use the compiler to verify that we're handling all possible cases correctly. This is particularly important for vendor specific protocols where we need to maintain compatibility with existing systems.

Performance optimization is often necessary for USB applications, particularly those handling high speed data transfers. Rust provides various tools for optimizing USB code, including careful memory alignment, efficient buffer management, and compile time optimizations. The zero cost abstractions ensure that our high level code compiles to efficient machine instructions.

Security considerations are important when implementing USB functionality, as USB devices can be attack vectors. Rust's memory safety helps prevent many common vulnerabilities, while we can implement additional security measures like input validation and protocol verification. This is particularly important for devices that handle sensitive data or provide system access.

Integrating USB functionality with other system components requires careful coordination. Rust's ownership and borrowing rules help manage shared resources safely, whether we're dealing with other peripherals, system state, or communication interfaces. We can create clear boundaries between USB handling code and other system components while maintaining efficient interaction.

As USB continues to evolve with new standards and features, Rust's strong typing and safety guarantees make it an excellent choice for implementing USB functionality in embedded systems. Whether building simple USB peripherals or complex composite devices, Rust helps ensure reliable and secure USB communication while maintaining high performance.

51. CAN Bus Implementation

The Controller Area Network (CAN) bus is a robust communication protocol widely used in automotive and industrial applications. Its reliability and deterministic behavior make it ideal for real time control systems and distributed networks. In embedded Rust, implementing CAN bus communication combines the protocol's inherent reliability with Rust's safety guarantees.

CAN bus operates on a message broadcast model where multiple nodes can communicate on the same bus. Each message has an identifier that determines its priority and allows nodes to filter which messages they process. Rust's type system helps us model this behavior safely, ensuring that message priorities and filtering rules are correctly enforced at compile time.

The fundamental unit in CAN communication is the frame, which contains the identifier, data length code, data bytes, and various control bits. In Rust, we can represent these frames using strongly typed structures that prevent invalid configurations:

A key aspect of CAN bus implementation is handling message arbitration, where multiple nodes may attempt to transmit simultaneously. The protocol resolves conflicts based on message identifiers, with lower values having higher priority. Rust's pattern matching capabilities make it straightforward to implement this arbitration logic while ensuring all cases are handled correctly.

Error detection and handling are crucial aspects of CAN bus communication. The protocol includes built in error detection mechanisms including CRC checking, bit stuffing, and various error states. Rust's error handling patterns allow us to represent and manage these error conditions clearly, helping prevent error propagation and ensure proper recovery:

Message filtering is an important feature in CAN implementations, allowing nodes to efficiently process only relevant messages. Rust's zero cost abstractions enable us to implement complex filtering rules without runtime overhead. We can create type safe filter configurations that are validated at compile time and compiled to efficient hardware filter registers.

When implementing CAN bus drivers, we need to handle both transmission and reception of messages asynchronously. Rust's async/await syntax provides elegant ways to manage these concurrent operations while maintaining safety. We can create efficient message queues and handle multiple pending transactions without risking data races or buffer overflows.

Hardware abstraction is essential for portable CAN implementations. Using Rust's trait system, we can define common interfaces for different CAN controllers while allowing hardware specific optimizations. This enables code reuse across different platforms while maintaining optimal performance:

Real time constraints are often critical in CAN applications. Messages must be transmitted and received within specific time windows, and priority inheritance must be handled correctly. Rust's predictable performance characteristics help ensure that these timing requirements are met consistently.

Buffer management requires careful consideration in CAN implementations. We need to handle both transmission and reception buffers efficiently while preventing overflow conditions. Rust's ownership system helps manage these buffers safely, ensuring that data is neither lost nor corrupted:

Many modern CAN implementations support additional features like CAN FD (Flexible Data Rate) which allows higher data rates and longer messages. Rust's type system helps us manage these extended capabilities safely, ensuring that we only use features supported by our hardware and other nodes on the network.

Testing CAN implementations presents unique challenges due to the distributed nature of the system. Rust's testing framework allows us to verify protocol handling in isolation while also supporting integration tests with actual CAN networks. We can create mock CAN buses for testing complex interactions without requiring physical hardware.

Security considerations are becoming increasingly important in CAN networks, particularly in automotive applications. While CAN itself provides limited security features, Rust helps us implement additional security measures like message authentication and input validation without compromising performance.

Debugging CAN communications often requires detailed analysis of message timing and sequencing. We can implement logging and monitoring features that capture this information without affecting the real time behavior of the system. Rust's conditional compilation features allow us to include extensive debugging capabilities that can be disabled in production builds.

Integration with other system components is often necessary in CAN applications. For example, we might need to coordinate CAN communication with sensor readings or actuator control. Rust's ownership model helps manage these interactions safely while maintaining real time performance:

Power management is important in many CAN applications, particularly in automotive systems. We need to handle sleep modes and wake up events correctly while maintaining network synchronization. Rust helps us manage these power state transitions safely, ensuring that all required operations are performed in the correct sequence.

As automotive and industrial networks continue to evolve, CAN remains a crucial protocol for reliable real time communication. Rust's combination of safety guarantees and zero cost abstractions makes it an excellent choice for implementing

CAN bus functionality in embedded systems. Whether building simple CAN nodes or complex distributed control systems, Rust helps ensure reliable and efficient communication while maintaining strict safety requirements.

The implementation of CAN bus in embedded Rust demonstrates how modern programming language features can enhance traditional embedded protocols. By combining Rust's safety guarantees with CAN's robust communication model, we can create reliable and efficient distributed systems that meet the demanding requirements of automotive and industrial applications.

52. Real-World IoT Architecture

Chapter 52 - Real World IoT Architecture

Building a robust Internet of Things architecture requires careful consideration of multiple layers, from hardware interfaces to cloud connectivity. In the context of embedded Rust, we can create reliable and secure IoT systems that scale effectively while maintaining strong safety guarantees throughout the entire stack.

The foundation of any IoT architecture begins at the device level, where sensors and actuators interface with the physical world. Rust's strong typing and ownership model help ensure that these hardware interactions are both safe and efficient. When designing the device layer, we need to consider power consumption, reliability, and local processing capabilities. Embedded Rust allows us to implement sophisticated edge computing functionality while maintaining strict resource constraints.

A typical IoT architecture implements a layered approach, starting with the physical layer where sensors and actuators operate. Above this sits the network layer, handling communication protocols like WiFi, Bluetooth, or cellular connections. The middleware layer manages data processing and device management, while the application layer provides user interfaces and business logic. Rust's flexibility allows us to implement each of these layers efficiently, with compile time guarantees preventing many common IoT security vulnerabilities.

Data collection and preprocessing at the edge is crucial for efficient IoT operations. Rather than transmitting raw sensor data, embedded devices often need to perform local analytics and filtering. Rust's zero cost abstractions enable efficient implementation of these preprocessing algorithms without sacrificing safety. We can create type safe data processing pipelines that minimize unnecessary network traffic while ensuring data integrity.

Gateway devices play a crucial role in IoT architectures, bridging local device networks with cloud services. These gateways often need to handle multiple communication protocols simultaneously while managing local device registration and security. Rust's async/await capabilities make it ideal for implementing these concurrent communication handlers, while its strong type system helps prevent protocol mismatches and data corruption.

Security must be implemented at every layer of the IoT architecture. At the device level, this includes secure boot processes, encrypted storage, and authenticated communication. Gateway devices need to manage device authentication, access control, and network security. Rust's security features help prevent common vulnerabilities like buffer overflows and data races, while its ecosystem provides robust cryptographic libraries for implementing additional security measures.

Message queuing and data buffering are essential components of reliable IoT systems. Devices may experience intermittent connectivity or varying network conditions, requiring local storage and intelligent retry mechanisms. Rust's ownership system helps manage these buffers safely, ensuring that data is neither lost nor corrupted during network outages or high load conditions.

Device management is another crucial aspect of IoT architecture. Systems need to handle device registration, configuration updates, and monitoring. Rust's serialization capabilities and type safe configuration management help ensure that device settings remain consistent and valid throughout the system's lifecycle. We can implement robust device management protocols that prevent configuration errors and maintain system stability.

Scalability considerations affect every aspect of IoT architecture. Systems must handle varying numbers of devices, different types of sensors, and changing network conditions. Rust's trait system allows us to create flexible abstractions that can adapt to different device capabilities while maintaining type safety. We can implement dynamic device discovery and configuration without compromising system reliability.

Real time requirements often come into play in IoT systems, particularly in industrial applications. Some sensors may need immediate response times, while others can tolerate longer latencies. Rust helps us manage these varying timing requirements through zero cost abstractions and predictable performance characteristics. We can implement priority based message handling and guarantee response times where needed.

Data persistence and storage strategies vary depending on the application requirements. Some devices may need local storage for offline operation, while others stream data directly to cloud services. Rust's ecosystem provides various storage options, from embedded databases to efficient serialization formats. We can implement appropriate storage solutions while maintaining data integrity and type safety.

Error handling in distributed IoT systems requires careful consideration. Network errors, device failures, and data corruption must all be handled gracefully. Rust's error handling patterns help ensure that all error conditions are properly addressed, preventing cascading failures and maintaining system stability. We can implement sophisticated error recovery mechanisms that keep the system running even when individual components fail.

Monitoring and diagnostics are essential for maintaining IoT systems in production. We need to track device health, network performance, and system metrics. Rust's logging and instrumentation capabilities allow us to implement comprehensive monitoring solutions without significant overhead. We can create detailed audit trails and performance metrics while maintaining system performance.

Integration with existing systems is often necessary in real world deployments. IoT systems may need to interface with legacy equipment, enterprise software, or third party services. Rust's foreign function interface and networking capabilities make it possible to implement these integrations safely and efficiently. We can create robust bridges between different systems while maintaining the safety guarantees that Rust provides.

Testing IoT architectures requires consideration of multiple factors including network conditions, device behavior, and system scale. Rust's testing framework supports both unit testing of individual components and integration testing of complete systems. We can create comprehensive test suites that verify system behavior under various conditions, helping ensure reliability in production deployments.

As IoT systems continue to evolve, architecture patterns must adapt to new requirements and technologies. Rust's strong safety guarantees and efficient performance characteristics make it an excellent choice for implementing these evolving architectures. Whether building small scale sensor networks or large industrial IoT systems, Rust helps ensure reliable and secure operation while maintaining flexibility for future growth.

53. Cloud Integration

Chapter 53 focuses on Cloud Integration for embedded Rust systems, building upon the architectural foundations established in previous chapters to connect IoT devices with cloud services securely and efficiently.

Cloud integration represents a critical component of modern IoT systems, enabling remote monitoring, data analysis, and device management at scale. When implementing cloud connectivity in embedded Rust applications, we must carefully consider data formats, communication protocols, and security implications while maintaining the language's safety guarantees.

The first consideration in cloud integration is choosing appropriate communication protocols. MQTT (Message Queuing Telemetry Transport) has become a de facto standard for IoT cloud connectivity due to its lightweight nature and publish-subscribe architecture. Implementing MQTT clients in embedded Rust requires careful handling of network states and message queues. The rumqttc crate provides a robust implementation that works well in resource-constrained environments while maintaining Rust's safety guarantees.

HTTP/HTTPS communication offers another pathway for cloud integration, particularly useful for REST API interactions. The embedded-nal trait system provides abstractions for network protocols, allowing us to implement HTTP clients that work across different network stacks. When implementing HTTP clients, we must carefully manage memory usage, as HTTP headers and payloads can consume significant resources on embedded devices.

Data serialization plays a crucial role in cloud integration. While JSON is widely used in cloud services, it may not be the most efficient choice for embedded systems. Alternative formats like CBOR (Concise Binary Object Representation) or Protocol Buffers offer more compact representations while maintaining good interoperability. Rust's serde ecosystem provides excellent support for these formats, allowing us to define type-safe serialization with minimal overhead.

Authentication and security become paramount when connecting to cloud services. OAuth 2.0 and JWT (JSON Web Tokens) are common authentication mechanisms, but implementing these protocols on embedded devices requires careful resource management. Rust's strong type system helps prevent common security vulnerabilities, while crates like jsonwebtoken provide efficient implementations of these standards.

Cloud providers often offer IoT-specific services with their own SDKs and protocols. Amazon AWS IoT Core, Microsoft Azure IoT Hub, and Google Cloud IoT Core each provide different approaches to device connectivity. When implementing these integrations in Rust, we often need to create safe abstractions around their C-based SDKs using the Foreign Function Interface (FFI). This requires careful handling of memory management and error conditions to maintain Rust's safety guarantees.

Device provisioning and certificate management form another crucial aspect of cloud integration. Embedded devices need secure storage for credentials and certificates, often implementing rotation policies for long-term security. Rust's type system helps ensure that sensitive credentials are handled safely, while traits can provide abstract interfaces for different storage backends.

Error handling in cloud communications requires robust retry mechanisms and fallback strategies. Network connectivity in IoT deployments can be unreliable, and our implementations must handle various failure modes gracefully. Rust's Result type and error handling patterns help ensure that all error conditions are properly addressed, preventing data loss and maintaining system stability.

Data buffering and queuing become essential when dealing with intermittent connectivity. Implementing local storage for outbound messages ensures that no data is lost during network outages. Rust's ownership system helps manage these buffers safely, while traits can provide abstract interfaces for different storage implementations, from simple RAM buffers to persistent flash storage.

Message batching and compression can significantly improve efficiency in cloud communications. By aggregating multiple messages and applying compression, we can reduce bandwidth usage and cloud ingestion costs. Rust's zero-cost abstractions allow us to implement these optimizations efficiently, while maintaining type safety and memory safety.

Rate limiting and throttling are often necessary to comply with cloud service limits and manage resource usage. Implementing token bucket algorithms or other rate limiting strategies helps prevent overwhelming cloud services during peak periods. Rust's precise control over timing and resource usage helps implement these mechanisms efficiently.

Monitoring cloud connectivity requires implementing heartbeat mechanisms and connection health checks. We need to track various metrics including latency, packet loss, and throughput to ensure reliable operation. Rust's timing primitives and async capabilities help implement these monitoring systems without significant overhead.

Testing cloud integrations presents unique challenges, as we need to verify behavior under various network conditions and error scenarios. Rust's testing framework allows us to create mock implementations of cloud services for testing, while traits provide abstract interfaces that can be implemented differently in test and production environments.

Device shadows or digital twins are common patterns in IoT cloud services, maintaining device state and desired configuration in the cloud. Implementing these patterns requires careful synchronization between device and cloud state. Rust's type system helps ensure that state transitions are handled correctly, while traits can provide abstract interfaces for different cloud providers' implementations.

Firmware updates over the cloud require careful implementation to ensure reliability and security. We need to verify firmware signatures, handle partial updates, and maintain system stability during the update process. Rust's safety features help prevent common update-related vulnerabilities, while its error handling ensures robust recovery from failed updates.

As IoT systems scale, cloud integration patterns must evolve to handle increasing numbers of devices and data volumes. Rust's efficient performance characteristics and strong safety guarantees make it an excellent choice for implementing these scalable cloud integrations, ensuring reliable and secure operation while maintaining flexibility for future growth.

54. Over-the-Air Updates

Over the Air (OTA) updates represent one of the most critical features in modern IoT systems, enabling remote maintenance, feature deployment, and security patches without physical access to devices. Implementing secure and reliable OTA updates in embedded Rust requires careful consideration of system architecture, memory management, and error handling to ensure devices remain operational throughout the update process.

The foundation of any OTA update system begins with a robust bootloader implementation. In Rust, we typically implement a two stage bootloader where the first stage remains immutable and handles basic hardware initialization, while the second stage manages the update process. This separation ensures that devices can recover from failed updates, as the first stage bootloader can always fall back to a known good state.

Memory partitioning plays a crucial role in OTA implementations. We need to maintain at least two firmware slots: one for the currently running firmware and another for receiving updates. Using Rust's const generics, we can define type safe abstractions for these memory regions, ensuring that write operations cannot accidentally corrupt the running firmware. Many systems implement an A/B partition scheme, where the device can boot from either partition and switch between them during updates.

Version management forms another essential component of OTA systems. We need to track both the currently running firmware version and any pending updates. Rust's strong type system helps prevent version comparison errors, while its serialization capabilities enable efficient storage and transmission of version information. Implementing semantic versioning allows for granular control over update compatibility and rollback policies.

The update process itself must be atomic to prevent partial updates from corrupting the system. We implement this using a state machine pattern in Rust, where each stage of the update process is explicitly modeled as a distinct state. The type system ensures that transitions between states follow valid paths, while error handling ensures that failed updates can be safely rolled back.

Firmware validation represents a critical security aspect of OTA updates. Before applying any update, we must verify its authenticity and integrity. Rust's cryptography ecosystem provides efficient implementations of common signature verification algorithms. We typically implement a chain of trust where updates must be signed with known keys, and signature verification occurs before any firmware is written to flash memory.

Delta updates can significantly reduce bandwidth requirements by transmitting only the differences between firmware versions. Implementing delta updates in Rust requires careful memory management, as we need to reconstruct the new firmware image from the existing firmware and the delta patch. Zero copy parsing techniques help minimize memory usage during this process.

Resource management during updates requires special attention. The update process must not interfere with critical system functions, and we need to ensure sufficient memory and power are available throughout the update. Rust's ownership system helps manage these resources safely, while async capabilities allow update operations to be interleaved with normal system operation.

Error handling during OTA updates must be particularly robust. Network failures, power interruptions, or hardware issues can occur at any point during the update process. Rust's Result type helps ensure all error conditions are handled appropriately, while the type system ensures that cleanup operations occur even in error cases through RAII patterns.

Progress reporting and logging during updates help maintain system observability. We implement progress tracking using Rust's trait system to abstract different reporting mechanisms, from simple LED indicators to detailed network telemetry. This information helps diagnose update failures and monitor fleet wide update campaigns.

Update scheduling and policies need to consider device operating conditions and network availability. We implement policy engines using Rust's trait system to abstract different scheduling strategies, from immediate updates to time window based approaches. These policies help ensure updates occur at appropriate times and maintain system stability.

Testing OTA implementations requires comprehensive simulation of various failure modes. Rust's testing framework enables creation of mock update servers and simulated network conditions. We implement test scenarios for power failures, network interruptions, and invalid firmware images to verify system recovery capabilities.

Security considerations extend beyond firmware validation. The update process must protect against replay attacks, version rollback attacks, and man in the middle attacks. Rust's type system helps implement secure protocols for firmware delivery, while its memory safety prevents common vulnerability classes in update handling code.

Bandwidth optimization becomes crucial when updating large fleets of devices. We implement compression and chunked transfer mechanisms to reduce network usage. Rust's zero cost abstractions allow efficient implementation of these optimizations without sacrificing safety or reliability.

Recovery mechanisms must handle various failure scenarios, including partially written firmware, corrupted bootloader configurations, or failed signature verifications. We implement multiple fallback paths and recovery strategies, using Rust's type system to ensure all failure modes are handled appropriately.

Update campaigns for device fleets require careful orchestration to maintain system stability. We implement phased rollout strategies and automatic rollback triggers based on device health metrics. Rust's async capabilities help manage multiple concurrent update operations while maintaining system responsiveness.

Post update verification ensures that devices function correctly after applying updates. We implement self test procedures that verify critical system functionality before committing to the new firmware. Rust's testing frameworks help automate these verification procedures across different device configurations.

Long term maintenance of OTA systems requires careful consideration of firmware storage requirements and update policies. We implement cleanup mechanisms for old firmware versions and maintain audit trails of update history. Rust's strong type system helps prevent accidental deletion of critical firmware components while managing these maintenance tasks.

55. Production Deployment Considerations

Production deployment for embedded Rust systems requires careful consideration of various factors to ensure reliable operation in real world environments. Moving from development to production involves addressing manufacturing processes, quality assurance, deployment strategies, and long term maintenance considerations.

Manufacturing processes for embedded Rust devices need to account for initial firmware programming and validation. Production line programming tools must be integrated into the manufacturing workflow, often utilizing programming jigs or custom fixtures. We typically implement custom programming protocols in Rust that can efficiently flash devices while performing validation checks. These protocols need to handle high volume programming while maintaining reliability and traceability.

Device provisioning represents a crucial step in production deployment. Each device requires unique identifiers, security credentials, and configuration parameters. Rust's strong type system helps prevent provisioning errors by enforcing strict validation of device specific data. We implement automated provisioning systems that can handle large scale device initialization while maintaining security and auditability.

Quality assurance processes must verify both hardware and software functionality. Automated test fixtures, implemented in Rust, can perform comprehensive functional testing of each device. These tests typically include verification of all peripherals, communication interfaces, and sensor calibration. Rust's testing framework enables creation of reproducible test sequences that can be executed efficiently in production environments.

Production firmware builds require special consideration. Debug features, verbose logging, and development tools must be disabled to optimize resource usage and enhance security. We implement build configurations using Rust's feature flags to control which capabilities are included in production builds. This ensures that production devices contain only necessary code while maintaining the ability to enable debugging features when needed.

Device serialization and tracking systems help maintain product traceability. Each device needs a unique serial number and production record. We implement database systems, often using Rust's serialization capabilities, to maintain manufacturing records including firmware versions, test results, and calibration data. This information proves invaluable for warranty service and product support.

Initial deployment strategies must consider how devices will be configured and commissioned in the field. Rust applications need robust initialization routines that can handle various deployment scenarios. We implement configuration workflows that guide installers through device setup while validating all parameters. These workflows must be reliable enough to handle real world conditions including poor network connectivity or power interruptions.

Production monitoring systems help track device health and performance in the field. We implement telemetry collection and analysis systems using Rust's async capabilities to efficiently process data from large device fleets. These systems help identify potential issues before they impact end users and provide valuable insights for product improvement.

Warranty and repair processes require special consideration. Service technicians need tools to diagnose and repair devices in the field. We implement diagnostic interfaces in Rust that provide detailed system information while maintaining security. These interfaces must be carefully designed to prevent unauthorized access while enabling legitimate repair operations.

Configuration management becomes crucial in production environments. Different product variants or regional requirements may need different firmware configurations. We implement configuration management systems in Rust that can track and validate device configurations across product lines. This ensures that devices receive appropriate settings while preventing configuration errors.

Production security measures must protect both devices and manufacturing infrastructure. We implement secure boot chains that prevent unauthorized firmware modifications, while also securing manufacturing tools and processes. Rust's security features help prevent common vulnerabilities in both device firmware and manufacturing systems.

Scaling considerations become important as production volumes increase. Manufacturing systems need to handle multiple production lines and high device volumes. We implement scalable architectures using Rust's concurrent programming features to manage multiple programming stations and test fixtures efficiently.

Documentation for production processes must be comprehensive and maintainable. We create detailed documentation covering manufacturing procedures, test specifications, and troubleshooting guides. This documentation needs regular updates to reflect process improvements and lessons learned from field experience.

Quality metrics and yield tracking help optimize production processes. We implement systems to collect and analyze manufacturing data, identifying potential process improvements or emerging issues. Rust's strong typing helps ensure data accuracy while processing large volumes of production metrics.

Environmental considerations affect production deployment decisions. Devices must operate reliably across temperature ranges and environmental conditions. We implement environmental testing procedures and collect performance data to verify proper operation under various conditions. This information helps refine product specifications and manufacturing processes.

Long term support planning must account for future maintenance needs. Production devices may require firmware updates, configuration changes, or repair services over their lifetime. We implement support systems that can maintain device functionality while managing obsolescence of components or development tools.

Supply chain management affects production deployment success. Component availability and lead times must be considered when planning production runs. We implement inventory tracking systems and work with suppliers to ensure consistent component quality and availability.

Production cost optimization requires careful balance of features and capabilities. We analyze resource usage and performance metrics to identify optimization opportunities without compromising reliability. Rust's zero cost abstractions help maintain efficient operation while preserving safety guarantees.

Regulatory compliance must be maintained throughout production deployment. Different markets may have varying certification requirements. We implement compliance testing procedures and maintain documentation to demonstrate conformance with relevant standards. This includes electromagnetic compatibility testing, safety certifications, and environmental regulations.

Field support systems help maintain deployed devices. We implement remote monitoring and diagnostic capabilities that help support teams resolve issues efficiently. These systems must balance providing necessary information with maintaining security and privacy of device data.

56. Certification and Compliance

Certification and compliance represent critical considerations when deploying embedded Rust systems in commercial products. Understanding and adhering to relevant standards ensures that devices can be legally sold and operated in target markets while maintaining safety and reliability.

Electromagnetic Compatibility (EMC) certification forms a fundamental requirement for electronic devices. Embedded Rust systems must demonstrate immunity to electromagnetic interference while limiting their own emissions. We implement design practices that minimize RF emissions, such as proper signal routing and filtering. Software considerations include careful timing of high frequency operations and management of switching noise. Testing procedures verify compliance with standards like FCC Part 15 in the United States or CE marking requirements in Europe.

Safety certifications ensure that devices operate without risking harm to users or property. Standards such as IEC 60730 for household appliances or IEC 61508 for industrial systems define requirements for software safety. Rust's memory safety features provide strong foundations for building certifiable systems. We implement safety monitoring functions that detect and respond to abnormal conditions. Documentation must demonstrate how software architecture and implementation details fulfill safety requirements.

Product specific certifications may apply depending on the application domain. Medical devices require FDA approval in the United States or CE marking under the Medical Device Regulation in Europe. These certifications involve extensive documentation of development processes and risk management procedures. We implement quality management systems that maintain traceability from requirements through testing and validation.

Security certifications become increasingly important for connected devices. Standards like Common Criteria or FIPS 140-3 define requirements for cryptographic implementations and security features. Rust's security guarantees help demonstrate compliance with these requirements. We implement security features following certification guidelines while maintaining documentation of threat models and mitigation strategies.

Environmental certifications address concerns about electronic waste and hazardous substances. Standards like RoHS restrict the use of certain materials in electronic products. While primarily affecting hardware design, software must support proper handling of end of life conditions and enable environmentally responsible disposal procedures. We implement power management features that extend device lifetime and reduce environmental impact.

Wireless certifications apply to devices using radio communications. Standards vary by region and frequency band, requiring careful attention to regulatory requirements. We implement software defined radio features that can adapt to different regional requirements while maintaining compliance with transmission power limits and channel assignments.

Industry specific standards may impose additional requirements. Automotive applications must comply with ISO 26262 for functional safety. Industrial control systems often require IEC 61131 compliance. We implement software architectures that support formal verification and validation procedures required by these standards.

Quality management certifications like ISO 9001 focus on development and manufacturing processes. These standards require documented procedures for software development, testing, and maintenance. We implement version control systems and change management procedures that maintain audit trails of all software modifications.

Documentation requirements for certification can be extensive. Technical construction files must demonstrate compliance with applicable standards. We maintain detailed documentation of software architecture, safety analysis, test procedures, and validation results. This documentation must remain current as software evolves through product lifetime.

Testing procedures for certification often require specialized equipment and expertise. We implement automated test suites that can reproduce certification tests and verify continued compliance. These tests must cover normal operation as well as fault conditions and error handling capabilities.

Compliance monitoring becomes an ongoing requirement after certification. Software updates must maintain compliance with original certifications or undergo recertification. We implement version control and deployment procedures that prevent unauthorized modifications that could affect certification status.

Regional variations in certification requirements necessitate flexible software designs. Different markets may have conflicting requirements or interpretation of standards. We implement configuration management systems that can adapt device behavior to maintain compliance across regions while minimizing code divergence.

Cost considerations for certification influence development strategies. Testing and documentation requirements can significantly impact project budgets. We implement reusable software components and test procedures that can be leveraged across multiple products to reduce certification costs.

Maintenance of certification status requires ongoing attention. Changes in standards or discovery of new security vulnerabilities may necessitate updates. We implement update mechanisms that can deploy certified patches while maintaining evidence of continued compliance.

Certification authorities may require access to source code or development tools for review. Rust's strong type system and memory safety features help demonstrate software reliability. We maintain development environments that can reproduce builds and test results for certification audits.

Third party components require careful evaluation for certification impact. External libraries or drivers must meet the same certification requirements as custom code. We implement dependency management procedures that track certification status of all software components.

Validation procedures must demonstrate compliance with certification requirements. We implement testing frameworks that can verify proper operation of safety features and security mechanisms. These tests must provide evidence of compliance that can withstand certification authority review.

Future certification requirements must be anticipated during development. Emerging standards for IoT security or artificial intelligence may impose new requirements. We implement flexible architectures that can adapt to evolving certification landscapes while maintaining existing compliance.

The certification process itself requires careful project management. Timelines must account for testing, documentation, and review cycles. We implement project tracking systems that monitor certification progress and highlight potential compliance issues early in development.

57. Advanced Project: Smart Home Controller

Advanced Project: Smart Home Controller represents an excellent opportunity to apply embedded Rust concepts in creating a sophisticated home automation system. This comprehensive project demonstrates how to integrate multiple sensors, actuators, and communication protocols while maintaining security and reliability.

The core of our smart home controller runs on a Raspberry Pi 4, leveraging Rust's strong type system and memory safety features. We begin by establishing a robust hardware abstraction layer that interfaces with various peripherals. The system architecture follows a modular design, allowing individual components to be developed, tested, and maintained independently.

Our controller implements multiple communication protocols to interact with different smart home devices. We utilize MQTT for primary device communication, implementing a broker that handles message routing between components. The system supports both WiFi and Ethernet connectivity, with automatic failover capabilities. Bluetooth Low Energy support enables direct interaction with compatible sensors and devices that don't require continuous network connectivity.

Security forms a critical aspect of the implementation. We utilize Rust's strong security guarantees while implementing additional layers of protection. All device communication is encrypted using TLS, with certificate based authentication for each connected device. The system implements secure storage for sensitive configuration data and credentials using hardware security features when available. Regular security audits are automated through integrated testing procedures.

The controller's user interface provides multiple access methods. A local web interface, built using the Rocket framework, enables direct device configuration and monitoring. Mobile applications can connect through a REST API, with GraphQL support for efficient data queries. Voice control integration allows natural language interaction through popular smart assistant platforms.

Environmental monitoring and control represent key functionalities. Temperature sensors throughout the home provide data for intelligent HVAC management. The system learns occupancy patterns and adjusts climate control accordingly, optimizing both comfort and energy efficiency. Air quality sensors monitor CO2, humidity, and particulate levels, triggering ventilation systems when necessary.

Lighting control demonstrates sophisticated automation capabilities. The system integrates with various smart bulbs and switches using both proprietary and standard protocols. Advanced scenes can be configured based on time of day, occupancy, and external conditions. Natural light sensors help maintain optimal illumination while minimizing energy consumption.

Security features include integration with cameras, motion sensors, and door contacts. The system implements intelligent detection algorithms that can distinguish between normal activity and potential security threats. Video processing runs locally using Rust based computer vision libraries, ensuring privacy while maintaining quick response times.

Energy management capabilities help optimize power consumption. The controller monitors real time energy usage through smart meter integration and individual device power monitoring. Machine learning algorithms identify patterns and suggest optimization strategies. Integration with solar power systems enables intelligent load balancing and storage management.

The system implements robust error handling and recovery procedures. All critical operations include timeout mechanisms and fallback modes. Automatic error reporting helps identify and diagnose issues quickly. The controller maintains local caching of essential functions to ensure basic operation continues even during network outages.

Data management includes both local storage and optional cloud integration. Time series databases store historical sensor data and system events. Analytics functions provide insights into system performance and usage patterns. Regular backups ensure configuration and historical data can be restored if necessary.

The update system ensures secure and reliable software maintenance. Over the air updates are cryptographically signed and verified before installation. The system maintains redundant bootloader configurations to recover from failed updates. Configuration changes are version controlled with rollback capabilities.

Extensibility remains a key design consideration. The system implements a plugin architecture that allows new device support to be added without modifying core functionality. A standardized API enables third party integrations while maintaining security boundaries. Documentation tools automatically generate API references from code comments.

Performance optimization ensures responsive operation even with numerous connected devices. The system utilizes Rust's zero cost abstractions to minimize overhead. Critical paths are optimized using async programming patterns. Resource intensive operations can be distributed across multiple cores.

Testing infrastructure validates system operation under various conditions. Integration tests verify proper interaction between components. Performance tests ensure responsiveness under load. Security tests attempt to identify potential vulnerabilities.

Automated testing runs as part of the continuous integration pipeline.

The project demonstrates practical implementation of embedded Rust patterns. Type safe interfaces prevent common programming errors. Memory safety guarantees eliminate entire classes of runtime bugs. Error handling patterns ensure graceful degradation when problems occur.

Documentation remains comprehensive throughout development. Architecture decisions are recorded with supporting rationale. API documentation includes usage examples. Deployment procedures detail hardware requirements and configuration steps. Troubleshooting guides help users resolve common issues.

This smart home controller project illustrates how embedded Rust enables development of complex, reliable systems. The implementation demonstrates practical application of security patterns, communication protocols, and user interface design. The resulting system provides a foundation for exploring advanced home automation capabilities while maintaining high standards for reliability and security.

58. Advanced Project: Industrial Control System

In this chapter, we explore the development of an industrial control system using Rust, demonstrating how the language's safety features and performance characteristics make it ideal for critical industrial applications. Our project focuses on creating a reliable control system suitable for manufacturing environments, process control, and industrial automation.

The system architecture centers around a fault tolerant design implemented on industrial grade hardware. We utilize a redundant configuration with hot failover capabilities, ensuring continuous operation even during hardware failures. The primary and backup controllers run on ruggedized computing platforms, each monitoring the other's health and ready to take over operations when necessary.

At the core of our implementation lies a deterministic real time scheduler. This component ensures precise timing for control loops and process monitoring. We leverage Rust's zero cost abstractions to implement priority based scheduling without runtime overhead. The scheduler maintains microsecond level precision while managing multiple control loops with different timing requirements.

Communication reliability forms a critical aspect of the system. We implement industrial protocols including Modbus, PROFINET, and EtherCAT using Rust's strong type system to prevent protocol violations. The communication stack includes automatic retry mechanisms and sophisticated error detection. Each protocol implementation undergoes rigorous testing to verify compliance with industrial standards.

The control logic implementation demonstrates advanced PID control algorithms. Multiple control loops operate simultaneously, managing various process parameters such as temperature, pressure, and flow rates. Each control loop implements anti windup protection and bumpless transfer between manual and automatic modes. The system supports both traditional PID control and more sophisticated model predictive control algorithms.

Data acquisition represents another crucial component. High speed analog and digital inputs capture process variables with precise timing. The system implements sophisticated signal conditioning and filtering algorithms to ensure accurate measurements. Calibration data for sensors is stored in a secure, redundant configuration database.

Safety features permeate every aspect of the design. The system implements multiple safety interlocks with redundant checking. Emergency shutdown procedures ensure equipment protection while maintaining process safety. All safety critical functions undergo formal verification using Rust's type system to prove correctness properties.

Our human machine interface provides operators with clear system visibility. The interface, built using a combination of web technologies and native display drivers, offers both local and remote access capabilities. Role based access control ensures operators can only perform authorized actions. The interface includes advanced visualization features for trend analysis and process optimization.

Alarm management follows ISA 18.2 standards for industrial alarm systems. The implementation includes sophisticated alarm filtering and prioritization logic. Operators receive clear guidance for alarm response through integrated procedure management. Historical alarm analysis helps identify recurring issues and optimize alarm thresholds.

The system implements comprehensive data logging and analysis capabilities. Process data is stored in a time series database optimized for industrial applications. Analytics functions provide insights into process efficiency and equipment health. The system supports export to common industrial data analysis tools while maintaining data integrity.

Equipment monitoring includes predictive maintenance capabilities. The system analyzes vibration patterns, temperature trends, and other indicators to predict potential failures. Integration with computerized maintenance management systems helps schedule preventive maintenance activities. Equipment lifecycle tracking provides insights into replacement planning.

Security measures protect against both external threats and internal mistakes. Network segmentation follows industrial security best practices. All communication uses strong encryption where supported by protocols. Access control extends to individual data points and control parameters. Regular security audits help identify potential vulnerabilities.

The system implements sophisticated batch control capabilities following ISA 88 standards. Recipe management allows flexible process configuration while maintaining product consistency. The batch execution engine handles complex sequences while providing detailed batch reporting. Electronic batch records maintain complete traceability.

Version control extends beyond software to include process configurations and control parameters. All changes are logged with full audit trails. The system supports automated validation of configuration changes against defined constraints. Rollback capabilities ensure quick recovery from problematic changes.

Diagnostic capabilities help quickly identify and resolve issues. The system includes comprehensive self diagnostic functions for both hardware and software components. Remote diagnostic capabilities enable expert support without site visits. Diagnostic data helps identify recurring issues and system bottlenecks.

Integration capabilities enable connection with enterprise systems. The implementation supports common industrial integration standards including OPC UA. Custom integration adapters can be safely implemented using Rust's strong type system. Data synchronization ensures consistency across connected systems.

Performance optimization ensures reliable operation under varying loads. Critical paths use lock free data structures to minimize latency. The system automatically adjusts sampling rates based on process dynamics. Resource monitoring helps prevent overload conditions.

Testing infrastructure validates system operation under various conditions. Automated testing includes both functional verification and performance validation. Hardware in the loop testing ensures proper operation with actual equipment. Fault injection testing verifies proper handling of various failure modes.

Documentation remains crucial for long term system maintenance. Detailed architecture documentation explains system organization and design decisions. Operating procedures cover both normal operation and emergency response. Maintenance documentation includes troubleshooting guides and common repair procedures.

This industrial control system project demonstrates how Rust's safety features combine with high performance capabilities to create reliable industrial applications. The implementation shows practical solutions for common industrial automation challenges while maintaining high standards for safety and reliability.

59. Advanced Project: Wearable Device

In this chapter, we delve into developing a sophisticated wearable device using Rust, showcasing how the language's capabilities are particularly well suited for resource constrained, battery powered devices that require reliable operation and real time processing capabilities.

Our wearable device project focuses on creating a health and fitness monitoring system that combines multiple sensors, wireless connectivity, and long battery life in a compact form factor. The design emphasizes power efficiency while maintaining responsive user interaction and reliable data collection.

The hardware platform centers around a low power microcontroller with built in Bluetooth Low Energy capabilities. We utilize the nRF52 series processor, which offers an excellent balance of processing power and energy efficiency. The system incorporates multiple sensors including an accelerometer for motion tracking, optical heart rate sensor, temperature sensor, and skin conductance sensor for stress monitoring.

Power management forms a crucial aspect of the implementation. We develop sophisticated power states that dynamically adjust system operation based on user activity and sensor requirements. The system switches between ultra low power sleep modes and active states, with careful management of sensor sampling rates and wireless communication intervals. Our implementation includes detailed power profiling to optimize energy consumption across different usage patterns.

The real time operating system implementation provides deterministic response while managing multiple sensor streams. We create a priority based task scheduler that ensures critical health monitoring functions maintain precise timing while allowing lower priority tasks like user interface updates to execute when resources are available. The scheduler implements sophisticated power aware task switching to minimize energy consumption during idle periods.

Sensor fusion algorithms combine data from multiple sources to provide accurate activity and health metrics. We implement a Kalman filter based approach for motion tracking that fuses accelerometer and gyroscope data. Heart rate validation combines optical sensor data with motion information to filter out movement artifacts. Temperature compensation algorithms ensure accurate readings across varying environmental conditions.

The Bluetooth Low Energy stack implementation focuses on reliable communication while minimizing power consumption. We create custom GATT services for health data transmission that optimize packet sizes and transmission intervals. The implementation includes robust connection management with automatic reconnection and data buffering during connection loss. Security features ensure health data remains private during transmission.

Storage management implements a circular buffer system for sensor data with automatic offloading to connected devices. The system optimizes flash memory usage to extend device lifetime while maintaining critical health data. Wear leveling algorithms distribute writes across the flash memory to prevent premature failure of frequently updated sectors.

The user interface combines a small e ink display with capacitive touch inputs. We implement an event driven interface system that responds to user interaction while maintaining low power operation. The display update system minimizes refresh operations to conserve power while ensuring important health alerts remain visible. Haptic feedback provides additional user interaction options without requiring visual attention.

Motion detection algorithms identify various activities and exercise patterns. We implement a machine learning based approach that runs efficiently on the limited hardware resources. The system recognizes common exercises and provides real time feedback on form and intensity. Step counting algorithms filter out false positives while maintaining accurate activity tracking.

Health monitoring features include continuous heart rate tracking with automatic detection of irregular patterns. The system implements configurable alarms for various health parameters. Advanced algorithms detect potential stress events based on combined sensor data. The implementation includes fall detection with automatic alert capabilities.

Error handling becomes particularly critical in wearable devices where user interaction may be limited. We implement a sophisticated error recovery system that attempts to maintain core functionality even when peripheral systems fail. The system includes automatic sensor recalibration when accuracy drifts and graceful degradation of features when battery power runs low.

Over the air update capabilities ensure the device can receive software improvements and bug fixes. We implement a secure bootloader that verifies firmware updates before installation. The update system includes automatic rollback capabilities if problems are detected after update. Delta updates minimize data transmission requirements for firmware updates.

Testing infrastructure validates system operation under various usage conditions. We create automated test suites that verify sensor accuracy and power consumption. Environmental chamber testing ensures reliable operation across temperature ranges. Drop testing validates physical durability of the assembled device.

Calibration procedures ensure accurate sensor readings across different users and wearing positions. The system implements automatic calibration routines that run during normal usage. Factory calibration data is stored in protected memory regions with checksums to detect corruption. Runtime calibration adjusts for changing environmental conditions.

The companion smartphone application provides extended functionality and data analysis. We implement a cross platform application using Rust based frameworks. The application includes sophisticated data visualization and trend analysis. Cloud backup ensures user data remains available even if devices are lost or damaged.

Documentation includes detailed assembly instructions and troubleshooting guides. We create user manuals that explain device operation and maintenance requirements. Developer documentation covers sensor integration and algorithm implementation details. Regulatory compliance documentation addresses various certification requirements.

This wearable device project demonstrates how Rust's strong safety guarantees and efficient resource utilization make it ideal for developing sophisticated wearable technology. The implementation shows practical solutions for common wearable device challenges while maintaining high standards for reliability and user experience.

60. Troubleshooting Common Issues

In embedded systems development, troubleshooting skills are essential for resolving the various issues that can arise during development, testing, and deployment. This chapter explores common problems encountered when working with embedded Rust applications and provides systematic approaches to diagnose and resolve them.

One of the most frequent challenges developers face is dealing with memory related issues. Even with Rust's strong memory safety guarantees, embedded systems can still experience problems due to stack overflow, heap fragmentation, or incorrect memory configurations. When troubleshooting memory issues, start by examining the memory map and stack usage analysis. Tools like probe run can help identify stack overflow conditions by monitoring stack watermarks during program execution. For heap related issues, memory allocator statistics and heap visualization tools can reveal fragmentation patterns or memory leaks.

Hardware initialization problems frequently manifest during development. When devices fail to start or operate correctly, systematic verification of clock configurations, peripheral initialization sequences, and power supply voltages is essential. Debug logging through UART or RTT can provide visibility into the initialization process. Always verify that fuse settings and boot configurations match the intended hardware configuration. Pay special attention to crystal oscillator startup times and power supply sequencing requirements.

Communication protocol issues require careful analysis of signal timing and data formats. When troubleshooting I2C, SPI, or UART problems, logic analyzers prove invaluable for capturing and analyzing signal patterns. Common issues include incorrect clock polarity, mismatched baud rates, or protocol timing violations.

Verify that pull up resistors are properly configured and signal levels meet the required voltage thresholds. For wireless protocols, packet sniffers can help identify communication errors or protocol violations.

Interrupt related problems can be particularly challenging to diagnose due to their asynchronous nature. When investigating interrupt issues, verify interrupt priority configurations and ensure proper interrupt handler registration. Race conditions can occur when interrupt handlers interact with main program flow. Use atomic operations and proper synchronization primitives to prevent data corruption. Debug logging within interrupt handlers should be used cautiously as it can affect timing and potentially mask underlying issues.

Real time performance problems often manifest as missed deadlines or inconsistent timing behavior. Profiling tools can help identify execution time bottlenecks and interrupt latency issues. Analyze critical paths through the application and verify that interrupt priorities are configured to meet timing requirements. Consider using hardware trace capabilities when available to capture detailed execution timing information. Memory access patterns and cache behavior can significantly impact real time performance.

Power consumption issues require careful analysis of device operating modes and peripheral configurations. Use current measurement tools to profile power consumption across different operating states. Verify that unused peripherals are properly disabled and clock gating is correctly configured. Sleep mode transitions should be carefully examined to ensure proper wake up behavior. Temperature monitoring during extended operation can reveal thermal issues that affect power consumption.

Debugging toolchain issues can impede development progress. When encountering problems with compilation, linking, or debugging, verify toolchain versions and compatibility. Ensure that target specifications match the actual hardware configuration. Link time optimization can sometimes cause unexpected behavior; try disabling it temporarily during troubleshooting. Keep detailed records of toolchain configurations to help identify when changes might have introduced problems.

Flash programming failures require systematic verification of programming parameters and hardware connections. Check that flash write protection is properly configured and verify programming voltages meet device specifications. Some devices require specific programming sequences or have timing requirements for flash operations. Maintain checksums of programmed data to verify integrity after writing.

Sensor integration problems often involve signal conditioning and calibration issues. Verify sensor power supply stability and signal ground connections. Analyze sensor data for noise patterns or drift that might indicate environmental interference. Implementation of proper filtering and calibration routines can help compensate for sensor non linearity or temperature effects.

Network connectivity issues in IoT devices require examination of both hardware and software configurations. Verify RF circuit matching and antenna placement for wireless devices. Network packet analysis can reveal protocol errors or timing issues. Implement proper error handling for network timeouts and connection failures. Consider environmental factors that might affect signal propagation.

When dealing with random or intermittent issues, environmental factors often play a significant role. Temperature variations, power supply noise, or electromagnetic interference can cause sporadic problems. Systematic testing across operating conditions can help identify environmental sensitivities. Consider implementing additional monitoring and logging to capture system state when intermittent issues occur.

Security related issues require careful analysis of potential attack vectors and vulnerability assessment. Verify proper implementation of secure boot processes and cryptographic operations. Analyze communication protocols for potential security weaknesses. Implement proper key management and secure storage of sensitive data.

Documentation plays a crucial role in troubleshooting. Maintain detailed logs of issues encountered and solutions implemented. Create troubleshooting guides that outline common problems and resolution steps. Document hardware configurations and software versions associated with specific issues. Share knowledge across development teams to improve overall system reliability.

Performance optimization issues often require careful balancing of multiple factors. Profile code execution to identify performance bottlenecks. Analyze memory access patterns and optimize data structures for embedded constraints. Consider trade offs between processing efficiency and power consumption. Implement performance monitoring to track system metrics over time.

When troubleshooting production devices, field diagnostics capabilities become essential. Implement logging systems that can capture relevant debug information without compromising system operation. Consider adding self test capabilities that can identify hardware or calibration issues. Provide mechanisms for secure remote diagnostics when possible.

The key to successful troubleshooting is maintaining a systematic approach and proper documentation of both problems and solutions. By understanding common issues and implementing robust debugging capabilities, developers can more efficiently resolve problems and improve overall system reliability.

61. Performance Profiling

Performance profiling is a critical aspect of embedded systems development that enables developers to optimize their applications for resource-constrained environments. Effective profiling helps identify bottlenecks, optimize memory usage, and ensure real time requirements are met consistently.

The foundation of performance profiling begins with establishing clear metrics and measurement methodologies. In embedded systems, key performance indicators typically include execution time, memory usage, power consumption, and interrupt latency. Hardware performance counters, when available, provide valuable insights into CPU utilization, cache behavior, and memory access patterns. Many modern microcontrollers include dedicated debug and trace hardware that can capture these metrics with minimal impact on system operation.

Execution time profiling requires careful instrumentation of code to measure critical paths and function execution durations. While traditional profiling tools may not be available for embedded targets, developers can implement lightweight timing mechanisms using hardware timers or cycle counters. For example, the cortex m core provides a cycle counter register that can be used to measure execution time with high precision. When implementing timing measurements, it's important to consider the overhead of the measurement itself and account for it in the analysis.

Memory profiling in embedded systems focuses on both static and dynamic allocation patterns. Static analysis tools can provide insights into code size and stack usage at compile time. Runtime memory profiling requires careful tracking of heap allocations and deallocations. Custom allocators can be implemented with built in profiling capabilities to track memory usage patterns, fragmentation, and potential leaks. Tools like memory maps and stack usage analysis help identify opportunities for optimization.

Power consumption profiling requires specialized hardware tools but provides essential insights for battery powered devices. Current measurement over time reveals power usage patterns during different operating modes. Correlating power measurements with code execution helps identify energy intensive operations. Profile different sleep modes and transition patterns to optimize overall power efficiency. Consider implementing power profiling capabilities directly in development boards to facilitate continuous monitoring during development.

Interrupt profiling is crucial for real time systems where predictable response times are essential. Measure interrupt latency and execution time to ensure system timing requirements are met. Profile interrupt handlers for potential priority inversions or excessive execution times. Tools like logic analyzers can capture interrupt timing patterns and help identify potential conflicts or timing violations.

Communication protocol profiling helps optimize data transfer efficiency and identify protocol overhead. Measure throughput and latency for different packet sizes and transmission patterns. Profile protocol state machines to identify potential bottlenecks or inefficient transitions. For wireless protocols, analyze radio usage patterns and power consumption during different communication states.

Cache behavior profiling becomes important when working with processors that include instruction or data caches. Analyze cache hit rates and identify patterns that cause cache misses. Profile memory access patterns to optimize data alignment and reduce cache thrashing. Consider implementing hardware trace capabilities to capture detailed cache behavior during critical operations.

Real time behavior profiling requires analysis of task scheduling and execution patterns. Measure task switching overhead and identify potential priority inversions. Profile mutex and semaphore usage to identify potential bottlenecks in task synchronization. Implement deadline monitoring to verify that real time constraints are consistently met.

When profiling embedded applications, it's essential to consider the impact of the profiling infrastructure itself. Instrumentation overhead can affect system timing and potentially mask or create performance issues. Implement configurable profiling levels that can be adjusted based on debugging needs. Consider using non intrusive profiling methods like hardware trace when available.

Advanced profiling techniques often combine multiple measurement approaches to provide comprehensive performance insights. Correlation of power consumption with execution patterns can reveal opportunities for optimization. Analysis of cache behavior in relation to memory access patterns helps optimize data structures and algorithms. Profile system behavior across different operating conditions to ensure consistent performance.

Automated profiling frameworks can help collect and analyze performance data over time. Implement continuous profiling capabilities that can track performance metrics during development and testing. Create visualization tools that help identify trends and potential issues. Consider implementing remote profiling capabilities for deployed devices to monitor real world performance.

Data analysis plays a crucial role in interpreting profiling results. Statistical analysis of performance metrics helps identify patterns and anomalies. Create baseline performance profiles for comparison during optimization efforts. Document performance requirements and regularly verify that they are being met through profiling data.

When optimizing based on profiling results, maintain a systematic approach. Focus on the most significant bottlenecks first and verify that optimizations don't introduce new problems. Consider the trade offs between different optimization strategies. Document optimization decisions and their impact on system performance.

Long term performance monitoring through profiling helps identify degradation over time. Implement mechanisms to collect performance metrics from deployed devices. Analyze trends to identify potential issues before they become critical. Use profiling data to inform future development decisions and optimization efforts.

The integration of profiling capabilities into the development workflow ensures consistent performance monitoring. Implement automated profiling as part of continuous integration testing. Create performance benchmarks that can be regularly verified. Maintain historical profiling data to track performance evolution over time.

Performance profiling remains an essential tool throughout the embedded system lifecycle. From initial development through deployment and maintenance, profiling data guides optimization efforts and helps ensure reliable system operation. Regular profiling and analysis help maintain system performance and identify potential issues before they impact operation.

62. Documentation Best Practices

Documentation best practices in embedded Rust development are essential for creating maintainable, collaborative, and long-lasting projects. Good documentation serves not only as a reference for current developers but also enables future maintainers to understand and modify the system effectively. This chapter explores comprehensive approaches to documenting embedded Rust projects.

Documentation in embedded systems presents unique challenges due to the intersection of hardware and software concerns. A well-documented embedded project should include both high-level architectural descriptions and low-level hardware interface details. Begin by documenting the system architecture, including block diagrams, data flow descriptions, and component interactions. This provides newcomers with a clear understanding of how different parts of the system work together.

Rust's built in documentation system, accessed through cargo doc, provides powerful tools for inline documentation. Use triple slash comments (///) for documenting public interfaces, and include examples that demonstrate proper usage. For embedded systems, these examples should include proper hardware initialization sequences, timing requirements, and any critical safety considerations. Document hardware dependencies explicitly, including required peripheral configurations and pin assignments.

Hardware interface documentation requires special attention in embedded systems. Create detailed pin mapping documents that specify how software interfaces correspond to physical hardware connections. Include timing diagrams for critical operations, especially when implementing communication protocols. Document register configurations and bit fields, particularly for custom peripheral implementations. Maintain accurate schematics and board layout documentation alongside software documentation.

Configuration management documentation helps users understand how to properly set up and modify system behavior. Document all configurable parameters, including their valid ranges and impacts on system operation. Include instructions for common configuration changes and their implications. For systems with multiple build configurations or feature flags, provide clear documentation of available options and their purposes.

Error handling documentation is crucial for embedded systems where debugging can be challenging. Document error conditions that can arise during operation and their recommended handling approaches. Include troubleshooting guides that help users identify and resolve common issues. Document system recovery procedures for various fault conditions. Maintain logs of known issues and their resolutions to help future troubleshooting efforts.

Real time behavior documentation should include timing requirements and constraints. Document interrupt priorities and their rationale. Include worst case execution time analyses for critical paths. Document task scheduling policies and their implications for system responsiveness. Provide clear guidelines for maintaining real time performance when modifying the system.

Memory management documentation helps prevent resource conflicts and overflows. Document memory layout including stack sizes, heap configurations, and special memory regions. Include guidelines for managing dynamic memory allocation in resource constrained environments. Document memory protection configurations and their implications for system security.

Security documentation becomes increasingly important as embedded systems connect to networks. Document security features and their proper usage. Include guidelines for secure configuration and deployment. Document update procedures and their security implications. Maintain records of security related changes and vulnerability assessments.

Testing documentation helps ensure system reliability and maintainability. Document test procedures including hardware setup requirements. Include automated test coverage reports and their interpretation. Document manual testing procedures that cannot be automated. Maintain test result histories to track system stability over time.

Build and deployment documentation enables smooth development workflows. Document development environment setup procedures including required tools and versions. Include step by step instructions for building and flashing firmware. Document continuous integration configurations and deployment procedures. Maintain release notes that track significant changes between versions.

API documentation should follow consistent patterns that make interfaces easy to understand. Use clear and concise function descriptions that specify preconditions and postconditions. Document thread safety considerations and concurrent access requirements. Include performance implications of different API usage patterns. Maintain backwards compatibility notes when interfaces change.

Power management documentation helps optimize battery life in portable systems. Document power consumption characteristics under different operating conditions. Include guidelines for implementing power saving features. Document wake up sources and their configuration requirements. Maintain power consumption benchmarks for different usage scenarios.

Debugging documentation aids in efficient problem resolution. Document available debug interfaces and their usage. Include common debugging procedures and tools. Document logging systems and their configuration options. Maintain troubleshooting guides for common development issues.

Consider documentation accessibility when organizing content. Implement clear navigation structures that help users find relevant information quickly. Include search functionality in documentation systems. Maintain consistent formatting and terminology throughout documentation. Consider generating multiple documentation formats for different user needs.

Version control practices for documentation are as important as those for code. Maintain documentation in version control alongside source code. Document significant changes in both code and documentation. Include documentation updates in code review processes. Maintain changelog entries that help track documentation evolution.

Regular documentation maintenance ensures continued relevance and accuracy. Schedule periodic reviews to verify documentation accuracy. Update documentation promptly when system changes occur. Archive outdated documentation appropriately. Maintain clear ownership and review processes for documentation updates.

Documentation tools and automation can improve consistency and maintenance efficiency. Use automated documentation generation tools where appropriate. Implement documentation testing to verify example code accuracy. Include documentation builds in continuous integration processes. Maintain tools for converting documentation between different formats as needed.

Remember that documentation serves different audiences with varying needs. Technical documentation helps developers understand implementation details. User documentation guides system operation and configuration. Maintenance documentation supports long term system support. Each audience requires appropriate detail levels and presentation styles.

Future maintainability depends heavily on documentation quality. Invest time in creating clear and comprehensive documentation during initial development. Maintain documentation quality through regular reviews and updates. Consider documentation impact when making system changes. Remember that good documentation reduces long term maintenance costs and improves system reliability.

63. Future of Embedded Rust

The future of embedded Rust stands at an exciting crossroads where safety, performance, and developer ergonomics converge to shape the next generation of embedded systems development. As we look forward, several key trends and developments are likely to define how Rust continues to evolve in the embedded space.

The embedded systems landscape is rapidly transforming with the proliferation of IoT devices, autonomous systems, and smart infrastructure. Rust's emphasis on memory safety without runtime overhead positions it perfectly to address the growing security concerns in these connected systems. We can expect to see increased adoption of Rust in safety-critical applications, where its compile-time guarantees provide significant advantages over traditional languages like C and C++.

One of the most promising developments on the horizon is the maturation of the embedded-hal ecosystem. As more hardware vendors provide official support for Rust, we'll likely see a broader selection of thoroughly tested, production-ready drivers and abstractions. This standardization will make it easier for developers to write portable code that works across different microcontroller families while maintaining the zero-cost abstractions that make Rust so appealing for embedded development.

Async/await support in embedded contexts is another area poised for significant growth. While already available in some forms, future developments will likely bring more sophisticated async runtimes optimized for resource-constrained environments. This will enable developers to write clearer, more maintainable concurrent code without sacrificing the deterministic behavior critical for embedded systems.

Real-time capabilities in Rust are expected to improve substantially. While Rust already offers powerful tools for building real-time systems, ongoing work in the compiler and standard library will likely provide even better guarantees for timing-critical applications. This includes more refined support for interrupt handling, improved timer abstractions, and better tools for analyzing and guaranteeing worst-case execution times.

The tooling ecosystem around embedded Rust development is rapidly evolving. We can anticipate more sophisticated debugging tools that leverage Rust's rich type system to provide better insight into program behavior. Integrated development environments will likely offer better support for embedded Rust development, including improved visualization tools for memory usage and real-time system behavior.

Machine learning and artificial intelligence at the edge represent another frontier where embedded Rust is likely to make significant inroads. As more computing moves to the edge, Rust's combination of performance and safety makes it an excellent choice for implementing machine learning inference engines on embedded devices. We can expect to see more libraries and tools specifically designed for this use case.

The automotive industry's growing interest in Rust could lead to significant developments in CAN bus implementations, automotive-grade safety certifications, and AUTOSAR compliance. This could pave the way for Rust to become a primary language in automotive software development, particularly as vehicles become more software-defined and connected.

Security features in embedded Rust will likely continue to evolve, with better support for hardware security modules, trusted execution environments, and secure boot implementations. The language's inherent safety guarantees, combined with these security-focused features, will make it an increasingly attractive choice for building secure IoT devices and industrial control systems.

Power management capabilities are expected to become more sophisticated, with better abstractions for managing different power states and optimizing energy usage. This will be particularly important as battery-powered IoT devices become more prevalent and energy efficiency becomes an even more critical concern.

Cross-platform development tools will likely improve, making it easier to develop and test embedded applications across different architectures and platforms. This could include better simulation tools, hardware-in-the-loop testing capabilities, and more sophisticated continuous integration pipelines specifically designed for embedded systems.

The adoption of Rust in commercial embedded products is likely to accelerate, leading to more real-world case studies and best practices emerging from production deployments. This practical experience will help shape the development of both the language and its embedded ecosystem, creating a positive feedback loop that benefits the entire community.

Memory management techniques in Rust will continue to evolve, with better support for specialized allocators and more sophisticated compile-time memory analysis tools. This will help developers make better use of limited resources while maintaining Rust's safety guarantees.

Real-time operating system implementations in Rust are likely to become more mature and feature-complete. We might see new RTOS designs that take full advantage of Rust's unique features, offering better safety guarantees while maintaining the performance characteristics required for real-time systems.

The educational ecosystem around embedded Rust will likely expand significantly. More universities and technical schools may adopt Rust in their embedded systems curricula, leading to a larger pool of developers comfortable with using Rust in embedded contexts.

Looking further ahead, we might see Rust influence the design of future microcontroller architectures. Hardware vendors might begin optimizing their designs to better support Rust's safety features and zero-cost abstractions, creating a more synergistic relationship between the language and the hardware it runs on.

The future of embedded Rust looks remarkably bright, with growing adoption, maturing tools and ecosystems, and expanding capabilities all pointing toward a more prominent role in embedded systems development. As the embedded world continues to evolve, Rust's combination of safety, performance, and developer ergonomics positions it well to meet the challenges of tomorrow's embedded systems.

64. Case Studies and Success Stories

Chapter 64 explores real world implementations and success stories of Rust in embedded systems, highlighting how organizations have successfully leveraged Rust's unique features to build reliable and secure embedded applications.

One of the most notable success stories comes from Microsoft, which has been gradually adopting Rust for security critical components. Their IoT division successfully rewrote several core networking components in Rust, resulting in a 70% reduction in reported security vulnerabilities and improved performance metrics. The team particularly praised Rust's ownership model for preventing common memory safety issues that had previously plagued their C++ codebase.

Google's Chrome OS team provides another compelling case study. They implemented several system level components in Rust, including parts of their firmware update mechanism. The team reported that Rust's strong type system and compile time checks caught numerous potential bugs before they could reach production. Their post mortem analysis showed that components written in Rust had significantly fewer runtime issues compared to equivalent C implementations.

In the automotive sector, Volkswagen's research division conducted a pilot project using Rust for vehicle control systems. They developed a prototype engine control unit (ECU) that demonstrated Rust's viability for safety critical automotive applications. The project highlighted how Rust's zero cost abstractions allowed them to maintain real time performance requirements while benefiting from higher level programming constructs. The team reported that the development time was reduced by approximately 25% compared to their traditional C based approach.

A particularly interesting case study comes from a medical device manufacturer that chose Rust for a new generation of insulin pumps. The project team cited Rust's memory safety guarantees as a crucial factor in their decision, given the life critical nature of their application. The resulting system passed FDA certification with fewer review cycles than their previous products, with auditors specifically noting the reduced risk profile due to Rust's safety features.

In the aerospace industry, a satellite communications company successfully deployed Rust in their ground station control systems. They reported that Rust's strong concurrency model significantly simplified the handling of multiple simultaneous satellite connections. The system has been running in production for over two years with zero memory related crashes, a marked improvement over their previous implementation.

The industrial automation sector provides several compelling examples of Rust adoption. A major robotics manufacturer implemented their motion control algorithms in Rust, achieving both better performance and improved safety guarantees. They reported that Rust's type system helped catch several edge cases in their inverse kinematics calculations during compilation, preventing potential runtime failures.

A smart home device manufacturer's experience offers insights into Rust's benefits for consumer IoT products. They rewrote their hub controller software in Rust, resulting in a 40% reduction in memory usage and improved response times. More importantly, they reported significantly fewer field incidents related to software crashes or memory corruption, leading to reduced warranty claims and improved customer satisfaction.

In the energy sector, a smart grid equipment manufacturer adopted Rust for their next generation power monitoring devices. They particularly praised Rust's ability to maintain deterministic performance while handling complex network protocols and real time measurements. The project lead noted that Rust's error handling forced them to explicitly consider failure modes, resulting in more robust error recovery mechanisms.

A particularly successful implementation comes from a weather monitoring system deployed in extreme environments. The development team chose Rust for its reliability and performance characteristics. After two years of operation in conditions ranging from arctic cold to desert heat, the systems have maintained continuous operation with zero software related failures. The team credited Rust's strict compile time checks for catching many potential issues that could have caused field failures.

Several startups have also reported significant success with Rust in embedded applications. One drone manufacturer implemented their flight control system entirely in Rust, citing the language's safety guarantees as crucial for their autonomous flight capabilities. They reported that development velocity actually increased once their team became comfortable with Rust's ownership model, as they spent less time debugging memory related issues.

In the agricultural sector, a precision farming equipment manufacturer successfully deployed Rust in their automated irrigation systems. They particularly valued Rust's strong support for concurrent programming, which helped them manage multiple sensor inputs and control outputs reliably. The system has been operating across hundreds of installations with minimal maintenance requirements.

A particularly interesting case study involves a scientific instrument manufacturer that used Rust for their latest spectroscopy equipment. They reported that Rust's performance characteristics allowed them to implement more sophisticated analysis algorithms directly on their embedded hardware, reducing the need for external processing. The development team noted that Rust's package ecosystem significantly accelerated their development process.

The success stories consistently highlight several key advantages of Rust in embedded systems. Memory safety guarantees, zero cost abstractions, and strong concurrency support are frequently cited as crucial benefits. Many organizations report initial hesitation due to Rust's learning curve, but nearly all indicate that the investment pays off through reduced debugging time and fewer production issues.

These case studies also reveal common patterns in successful Rust adoption. Most organizations started with smaller, well defined components before expanding to larger systems. They invested in team training and accepted initial productivity impacts during the learning phase. Many report that having experienced Rust developers mentor team members was crucial for successful adoption.

The financial impact of Rust adoption is also noteworthy. Multiple organizations report reduced maintenance costs, fewer warranty claims, and faster time to market for new features once their teams became proficient with Rust. Several noted that while initial development might take longer, the reduction in debugging and support costs more than compensated for the upfront investment.

These success stories demonstrate that Rust has matured into a viable option for production embedded systems across a wide range of industries. The consistent themes of improved reliability, better security, and maintained or improved performance suggest that Rust's adoption in embedded systems will continue to grow as more organizations recognize these benefits.

65. Moving Forward with Embedded Rust

As we conclude our exploration of embedded Rust development, it's important to consider the path forward and how to continue growing in this dynamic field. The embedded systems landscape is constantly evolving, and Rust's role in this ecosystem continues to expand and mature.

One of the most promising areas for continued growth is in the development of more sophisticated embedded frameworks and abstractions. While the current embedded HAL ecosystem provides excellent foundational support, there's significant opportunity for developing higher level abstractions that maintain Rust's zero cost guarantees while providing more ergonomic APIs. Developers looking to advance their skills should consider contributing to these efforts, as they represent the future of embedded Rust development.

Staying current with hardware developments is crucial for embedded Rust developers. New microcontroller families and architectures are continuously being released, each offering unique capabilities and challenges. The Rust ecosystem needs developers who can help maintain and expand support for these platforms. Consider choosing a specific hardware platform or vendor and becoming an expert in implementing Rust support for their devices.

Professional development in embedded Rust should focus on both deepening technical knowledge and broadening practical experience. This might involve taking on increasingly complex projects, perhaps starting with simple sensor interfaces and progressing to full featured IoT devices or real time control systems. The journey from basic GPIO manipulation to implementing complex communication protocols and real time operations represents a natural progression in expertise.

Security will continue to be a critical focus area for embedded systems development. Rust's safety guarantees provide an excellent foundation, but developers should stay informed about emerging security threats and best practices. This includes understanding secure boot implementations, encryption protocols, and secure update mechanisms. The future of IoT depends on devices that can maintain their security integrity throughout their operational lifetime.

Community involvement represents another crucial aspect of moving forward with embedded Rust. The language's ecosystem thrives on community contributions, from documentation improvements to new crate developments. Consider participating in Rust working groups, particularly those focused on embedded development. These groups often drive important initiatives that shape the future of embedded Rust development.

Performance optimization remains a critical skill for embedded developers. While Rust provides excellent performance characteristics out of the box, understanding how to fully leverage these capabilities requires continuous learning. This includes staying current with new compiler optimizations, understanding hardware specific performance characteristics, and mastering advanced profiling techniques.

Real time systems development presents particular challenges and opportunities for embedded Rust developers. As more organizations adopt Rust for safety critical systems, the demand for developers who understand both Rust's safety guarantees and real time constraints will grow. This intersection of safety and performance represents a particularly valuable skill set.

Cross platform development skills become increasingly important as embedded systems grow more complex. Many modern embedded applications involve multiple computing platforms working together, from microcontrollers to single board computers to cloud services. Understanding how to effectively architect and implement these distributed systems in Rust represents a valuable expertise.

The Internet of Things continues to expand, creating opportunities for developers who understand both embedded systems and network connectivity. Future embedded Rust developers should focus on understanding network protocols, wireless communications, and cloud integration patterns. This includes mastering Rust's async capabilities and understanding how to apply them in resource constrained environments.

Certification requirements for embedded systems are becoming more stringent, particularly in regulated industries like automotive, medical, and aerospace. Developers should understand how to develop and document code that meets these requirements. This includes mastering formal verification techniques and understanding how to leverage Rust's type system to provide stronger correctness guarantees.

Testing methodologies for embedded systems continue to evolve. Moving forward, developers should focus on building comprehensive test suites that cover both software functionality and hardware interaction. This includes unit tests, integration tests, and hardware in the loop testing. Understanding how to effectively test embedded systems represents a crucial skill for professional development.

Documentation remains a critical aspect of embedded development. As systems become more complex, the ability to clearly document both code and systems architecture becomes increasingly important. This includes both technical documentation and user facing documentation. Consider developing expertise in documentation tools and techniques specific to embedded systems.

Continuous integration and deployment practices for embedded systems present unique challenges. Understanding how to set up effective CI/CD pipelines for embedded projects, including hardware testing and firmware deployment, represents an important area for professional development. This includes mastering tools for automated testing and deployment of embedded software.

Power management and optimization will continue to be crucial considerations for embedded systems. As devices become more sophisticated, understanding how to effectively manage power consumption while maintaining functionality becomes increasingly important. This includes mastering both hardware and software techniques for power optimization.

The future of embedded Rust development looks particularly promising in several emerging fields. Edge computing, artificial intelligence on embedded devices, and advanced sensor fusion applications represent areas where Rust's combination of performance and safety make it particularly well suited. Developers should consider focusing on these emerging applications as they represent significant growth opportunities.

Looking forward, the embedded Rust ecosystem will likely continue to mature and expand. This includes better development tools, more sophisticated debugging capabilities, and improved support for various hardware platforms. Staying current with these developments and contributing to their advancement represents an important aspect of professional growth in embedded Rust development.

Success in embedded Rust development requires a commitment to continuous learning and improvement. This includes not only keeping up with language developments but also staying current with hardware trends, security practices, and industry standards. The field of embedded systems continues to evolve, and successful developers must evolve with it.

Don't miss out!

Visit the website below and you can sign up to receive emails whenever James Oakton publishes a new book. There's no charge and no obligation.

https://books2read.com/r/B-A-HVDVC-JPKIF

BOOKS 2 READ

Connecting independent readers to independent writers.

About the Publisher

Northwood Lore Books is an independent imprint dedicated to producing accessible, thought-provoking content through the use of advanced content generation systems. All books published under this imprint are created for educational or entertainment purposes only. Authors listed under this imprint use pen names and are not subject-matter experts. Accordingly, no material should be interpreted as financial, legal, medical, or professional advice. The information provided is general in nature, subject to change, and may not reflect the most current data or guidance. Readers are encouraged to consult official sources or qualified professionals before making decisions based on the content herein.

www.ingramcontent.com/pod-product-compliance
Lightning Source LLC
LaVergne TN
LVHW052245200926
848481LV00002B/279
* 9 7 9 8 2 3 0 7 6 5 2 6 4 *